FIRMLY ROOTED
Faithfully Growing

Principle-Based Ministry in the Church

David Horner

Firmly Rooted, Faithfully Growing
Principle-Based Ministry in the Church

Providence Communications
6339 Glenwood Avenue, Raleigh, NC 27612-2638

ISBN: 0-9740963-0-X

1. Church 2. Religious Aspects – Christianity

Acknowledgments

To my wife Cathy
Whose love, sacrifice, and support
made this book possible;

To the wonderful congregation and pastoral staff of
Providence Baptist Church
Whose lives demonstrate the truth
of these principles;

To two gracious co-laborers and friends
Whose encouragement and personal investment
Have readied this project for publication –
Diana Mattix, Jennifer Sharpe

Table of Contents

Table of Contents

Introduction

"So, is what I see here intentional, or is it just happening in spite of everything?" One Sunday not too many years ago, a gentleman asked me that question – one of the most penetrating questions I have ever been asked by a visitor to our church. I can honestly say that I was not sure how to take it. Was he implying that we had no idea what we were doing and yet somehow God had chosen to bless us? Was he suggesting that if we had a "real pastor" this ministry could really take off? Should I be highly insulted or deeply humbled by what he was asking? After a split second for all kinds of questions to race through my mind, I had to laugh out loud and reply, "Well, that is a loaded question! What do you really want to know?"

He responded by saying, "I enjoyed the morning service, and I want to know if there is a foundation beneath the surface that accounts for what I have seen." This visitor cut through the outward appearance and got to the root of how we ought to be thinking as a church. Does this church know why it exists and is it functioning according to a plan worthy of its calling? Over the next several minutes, we had an exhilarating discussion about the purpose of the Church in general and the specific focus of God's calling for Providence Baptist Church.

If someone asked you that question about your church, what would you say? Even though the majority of people in churches have no interest in delving into these kinds of issues, every member needs to know that someone has taken the time to address the most fundamental questions of why the Church exists. Therefore, it is critical that the pastor and church leaders have a basic understanding of the purpose of the church and the principles upon which that purpose has been founded.

Nothing is more frustrating for me as a pastor than to reason with leaders in the church who are such pragmatists that they are not interested in the "why." All they want to know is what to do next. Granted, good leaders should want to know what to do next, but they also need to be able to understand why that is important. What pastor would not be frustrated to find a first-time visitor asking questions that his own leadership does not consider relevant? When the ministry and growth of a congregation can be explained only by external factors, such as location, programs, and facilities, I have serious concerns for its future.

Nearly everyone has an opinion about what should be happening in the church they attend. Yet very few people, even those who are committed church members, understand either what is going on or what should be going on. We face a generation of churches in serious trouble because they have no idea what God wants them to be.

Why another book about church growth?

You may be asking why we need another book about "church growth." I believe there are several reasons:

1. **The Church was not created for the sake of its members or even for the good of the human race.**
    The Scriptures are clear. God has ordained that the Church serve as the Bride for His Son, and Christ's wedding day will come. Since the delay has been so long, some have stopped looking for His coming and have allowed the Bride to become sloppy and careless in both her appearance and in her character. God assures us that the wedding is coming, sooner than ever: "Let us rejoice and be glad and give the glory to Him, for the marriage of the Lamb has come and His bride has made herself ready" (Revelation 19:7). How awful it would be if the Church is unprepared for His coming, ill-equipped for that glorious day!

Introduction

Jesus Christ died for His Church, sacrificing Himself so that He might present her to Himself as a "holy and blameless" Bride "without spot or wrinkle or any other blemish" (Ephesians 5:25-27 NIV; see also Ephesians 4:24). He delights in her purity and has committed His power to bring her to completeness. What He has begun will never stop until the mission is accomplished, for His Bride will be complete.

The apostle Paul said, "For I am confident of this very thing, that He who began a good work in you will perfect it until the day of Christ Jesus" (Philippians 1:6). Many churches have lost sight of this and have forgotten who they are. Yet as Lord of all, He deserves what He desires and should not have to settle for a Bride that remains content to go her own way, disregarding His plans and purposes.

2. Many churches are *not* healthy.

Although America has an abundance of churches, the majority are suffering from the ravages of our times. Many once vital ministries are being forced to disband and close their doors due to declining attendance or the divisive impact of internal power struggles. Church members bicker among themselves, pastors defend themselves against church boards, charter members fight the influx of "new blood" in order to resist change at all costs, and so the infighting stifles all hope of growing in Christ.

The influence of radical elements within the church growth movement[1] has also introduced confusion and discontent on many fronts. For example, ambition has crept in under the guise of "striving for excellence" and "seeking God's best." Ungodly practices and worldly behavior have infiltrated churches at nearly every level with both members and leaders falling into disgrace due to unrestrained standards of personal character and untaught principles of personal modesty, morality, and purity.

Congregations are becoming more anthropocentric than theocentric or Christocentric. They prefer to be entertained by the quality of the

---

1 For further discussion of the church growth movement, please see the appendix entitled "A Misguided Emphasis on Church Growth."

production rather than awed by the majesty of God, more impressed by numbers than impacted by holiness. Church staffs extol models of business management more than models of spiritual maturity, react to urgent needs instead of remaining proactive to priority needs, and are driven by the bottom line rather than called to eternal purposes. Whenever these symptoms arise, we can be sure that the spiritual health of the body of Christ is at stake. Our calling is to take care of the *depth* of the ministry and leave the *breadth* to the Lord.

Sadly, few pastors are prepared to face these problems. They have not been equipped to help their churches rediscover their reason for being and recapture the contagious enthusiasm present in churches that understand God's plans. But what a hope we can have if we accept what God said about His people in Jeremiah 29:11: "For I know the plans that I have for you, declares the Lord, plans for welfare and not for calamity to give you a future and a hope." Unhealthy churches need to know what those plans are, just as healthy churches need to implement those plans consistently and intentionally.

3. **Some churches recognize the symptoms of poor congregational health but apply trendy solutions rather than turning to God's Word.**

A few years ago, a neighboring congregation ran into hard times. Attendance and giving were down. Despite being located in a high-growth area, they languished in their declining condition while surrounding churches enjoyed success. Something needed to be done. Unfortunately, the church did not choose to review what the Bible says about what a church is supposed to look like, what kinds of churches please Christ the most, and how the Bride can be best prepared for the coming of the Bridegroom.

Instead, this congregation chose to do what many congregations across the nation are doing these days. They went shopping for a solution and found it in a ministry style being promoted by a large church in another part of the country. Without evaluating the suitability of the ministry approach to their core values,[2] spiritual gifts, leadership skills, and most importantly, to God's Word, the church launched into a program that was on the cutting edge but was ill-suited for them. Sadly, the result was that they soon folded – just as quickly as David would have collapsed had he battled with Goliath dressed in the wrong suit, the armor of Saul.

Applying a few new ideas from denominational headquarters and grasping for the latest trends on the church growth circuit can never substitute for some hard work before an open Bible and a heart searching for wisdom and discernment from God. Although this book does not pretend to have all the answers, it does offer a process for you to follow to determine what God would have your church do to fulfill His calling.

4. People have no vision of what the Church can be.

Proverbs 29:18 KJV states, "Where there is no vision, the people perish." Congregations need to be able to envision God's intent. They need to understand His model of the Church and not embrace some traditional model handed down from the previous generation, or a newer one based on rampant concessions to culture. They want to see the Church as Christ wants it – a holy Bride! Nothing else will do once they have seen what Christ desires.

Has your church lost that sense of vitality and excitement for ministry that was once present? Does your congregation have a dream for what they expect to see the Lord do in their lives? What is the vision for your church? What is your passion and burden for God?

People need a vision that arises from a balanced examination of God's Word and a plan to move the principles from the pages of the Scriptures into the lives of the congregation. Churches need to lay out a clear vision that sets the course for the people to follow. People

---

2 For further discussion of core values, please see the appendix entitled "Core Values of Providence Baptist Church."

need a godly vision, one that comes from the Lord and not from the ambitions of pastors or congregations in their pursuit of developing a successful church. If we allow the Lord to define what "successful" means, then godly vision is never a problem. But when the vision comes from people who want to achieve greatness to prove their ability, this vision will kill the work of the Holy Spirit and divide men and women with competing ambitions.

In addition, this vision must be derived from a careful application of biblical principles that takes into account not only *what* the Lord wants done but *how* He wants it done. This difference will be discussed later in terms of the *content* of the ministry as shaped by the *character* of the ministry. In other words, if the church is operating in the power of the Holy Spirit according to the principles of God's Word, what would the results look like? [3]

This book will offer you a way to clarify your vision for your church so that the people can thrive and prosper with joy in fulfilling their calling as the body of Christ.

Who will benefit from this book?

I have spoken to hundreds of my fellow pastors during my years in the ministry, and very few have any recollection of learning these kinds of principles in the formal training process. Most of us wish that we could have spent more time studying the integration of biblical and theological studies with the practical aspects of ministry. We often feel overwhelmed by the relentless need to figure out how to lead groups of Christians who have called us to be their pastors and want us to help them learn how to live their lives for Jesus Christ.

As a result, I wrote this book with those who train pastors in mind. I hope that they will find this book to be helpful and applicable for their

---

3 For further discussion of formulating an approach to ministry, please see the appendix entitled "Asking the Right Questions."

students, whether they teach in the context of pastors' conferences or seminars, in a local church setting, or in a formal training center like a Bible institute, college, or seminary.

I also pray that this book will be a trusted resource for my fellow pastors as they work through these issues in their own congregations. I hope that the foundations outlined here will bear much fruit and encourage them to consider the implications of these principles for the ministry years ahead. As a pastor, I have a great love for other pastors and have made a commitment to exchange ideas with them that will serve all of us well as we seek to become better shepherds of the flocks entrusted to us. Consequently, I want to invite pastors to reflect on these principles, teach them to their congregations, and implement them as the Lord takes these basic truths and reshapes them to fit the specific needs of their churches.

I would also encourage pastors to share this book with their church leaders and church members. If leaders do not know why their church is moving in a certain direction, how can they lead? At every level of leadership in the church, leaders need to understand and own these principles in order to function in a capacity consistent with their calling to teach and equip people to follow Christ. If different purposes are being pursued by various leaders within the church, the disorder and confusion caused among those called to follow can be discouraging and frustrating. On the other hand, if we take a journey in the same direction, care about the same issues, abide by the same processes, embrace the same values, and look forward to the same destination, it can be a wonderful experience! This can only happen when all the leaders agree on why they do what they do, what they are to do, and how they are to do it.

To many people, church membership means nothing more than another line on a resumé of civic involvement. Yet every believer ought to know why being an active member of a local congregation means something important and presents one of the greatest challenges in the Christian life. This new understanding of what the Church is all about will give value to a privilege that has been woefully devalued in our culture. As church members see the glorious purpose of the Church and recognize the role God has for them in accomplishing that purpose, a new level of enthusiasm and excitement will emerge in their hearts.

A Personal Adventure

This book represents my search for answers in the Bible and describes how God used His Word to teach me about the purpose of the Church. I owe a debt of gratitude to the Father for allowing me to confront my ignorance by digging into His Word and finding ways to do what is important to Him.

I have profited more than anyone else ever will simply because I have had to wrestle with concepts that were over my head. I have had to think through issues that others may have already settled but still called for closure in my own mind. I had to take these steps before I could pour my life into a course of action that would keep me wholly occupied until I died or Jesus returns. I cannot imagine giving everything to a plan for my life that I was not sure could withstand careful scrutiny. If my life was to be invested in ministry, I wanted that investment to be a sure thing. That is why I have put so much of myself into learning and teaching the biblical truths that I now share with you.

Maybe you will find yourself disagreeing with something I have written or even feel forced to defend biblically another way of viewing a matter important to you and to the church you serve. If so, then I have succeeded in making you think. What I really want is for churches and their members to step away from their routines and to consider the greatness of our calling, the magnitude of the endeavor we have begun in Christ. I hope you will take this opportunity to think long and hard about the true nature of the Church and its ministry. May He take your heart and mind far beyond the written words of this book and open your eyes to all He wants to do in you and in His Church. Together we will explore biblical principles that outline the following:

- the roots (foundation) of a healthy church

- the biblical content of ministry (exaltation, evangelism, and edification)

- the godly character of ministry (structural and spiritual integrity of the church)

The adventure of finding out what the Lord has in store awaits us. We cannot say with certainty what each new turn will bring; after all, "No eye has seen, no ear has heard, no mind has conceived what God has prepared for those who love Him" (1 Corinthians 2:9 NIV). But as you approach this study, let the Lord show you a fresh vision of His Church, the Bride of Christ. It is my hope and prayer that you will interact with each chapter with your Bible open and with an attitude that longs not to see and criticize the Church as it is, but to see it for what it can be and what it will be through Jesus Christ.

Section One

THE ROOTS OF A HEALTHY CHURCH

*So that Christ may dwell
in your hearts through faith...
rooted and grounded in love.
Ephesians 3:17*

A church is only equipped for its ministry
as it is equipped by the Word of God.

All Scripture is inspired by God

and profitable for teaching, for reproof,

for correction, for training in righteousness;

so that the man of God may be adequate,

equipped for every good work.

2 Timothy 3:16-17

Rooted in God's Principles

How many churches have you visited in your lifetime? Thinking back, I must have been in at least a hundred – either as a member of a youth ministry team during high school, a participating church member, a teacher on mission trips or conferences, a visitor during a vacation or sabbatical, or as part of the pastoral staff team. I have been in churches that held to such liberal views of God and His Word that I was nervous being in the same room while heresy polluted the hearts and minds of those present. Other churches were bound by the chains of legalistic teaching and choked by an iron grip of negativism and joylessness.

But I have also had the privilege of worshiping and joining in ministry with those who sincerely loved and followed Christ obediently, yet expressed their love for Him in ways far different than mine. The conclusion I have drawn from these experiences simply bears out what I already knew from the Scriptures: God created each of us to reflect His image but chose to do so with incredible diversity.

Several years ago I had the chance to put that premise to the test all in one day. An opportunity to minister in South Africa arose, and I jumped at the chance. One Sunday during my trip, I was scheduled to preach in three different churches. In the morning, I was the guest of a church with a very expressive style of worship. People not only demonstrated their joy verbally in songs and shouts of praise, but found great delight in leaping, dancing, and waving colorful scarves in the air as they ran up and down the aisles with abandon. The atmosphere was in no way irreverent or inappropriate, but still very different from what I was used to experiencing in corporate worship!

The second worship experience came in the afternoon in a Zulu congregation conducted in their language. During the time I was present (the service had begun long before our group arrived and continued long after we left), we worshiped with special music selections from the youth choir, testimonies from the congregation, and lots of enthusiastic congregational singing. The service included the dedication of several children, the ordination of some church leaders, a time of prayer for healing the sick, and a message from their pastor as well as a sermon I delivered with the help of an enthusiastic translator.

We even watched in amazement as a woman had to be removed from the service for disrupting the proceedings with what were described to me as demonic outbursts. All of this transpired over the course of about two hours. But don't get the idea that this was some kind of circus with no semblance of order. A genuine sense of the Lord's presence was present in this cramped, rustic, cinderblock and tin building, among a loving and warm people who demonstrated a deep humility before the Lord and an authentic interest in giving glory to Him with all their hearts.

A few hours later, I participated in my third worship service of the day, a genteel service of warmth and dignity in an Anglican congregation. These fellow brothers and sisters in Christ had a deep passion for their Savior and a profound reverence for the God of glory. A sensitive and beautiful time of worship in song preceded my message, and a hunger for the Word was evident in the faces of the people as I stood to preach. Once again, I stood in awe of how God opened the hearts of people to the teaching of His Word, who received what I shared with overwhelming gratitude.

Three churches, three worship services, three unique groups of people, all showering their Lord with praise, receiving His Word with gratitude, and demonstrating His love in the sweetness of the fellowship before and after the worship times. I was deeply moved that God had given me a glimpse of a day in the life of His Church. Heaven rejoiced in each place with each style of worship because Jesus Christ was exalted to the glory of His Father. When I returned home, I was more determined than ever to celebrate the uniqueness and diversity of the body of Christ by zeroing in on what He wanted to develop in the church He had called me to serve.

Each church follows a unique course prescribed for it by the Lord. No two churches are alike in every way because each one is composed of different people with different gifts and callings. For years I have taught that God has a special calling for each congregation, a calling for it to become all He created it to be. The unique character of any given congregation emerges only as the spiritual gifts and interests of the people are identified and employed. Now more than ever, I am convinced that He wants churches to let Him shape their ministry, along lines best suited for their unique growth, as places of praise among people who live solely for His glory (1 Corinthians 12:11, 18, 24).

However, if we want to serve Christ faithfully as His people, biblical principles cannot be compromised. Certain criteria based on unchanging principles are essential if a church is to serve Christ effectively. After many years of study and practice, I believe strongly that the body of Christ functions best when it understands itself as a principle-based ministry. The Church can never become what Christ designed it to be unless its identity is based on principles discovered in the Bible, a resource given to us by God for just that purpose.

Discovering God's Principles for Healthy Churches

When Providence began in 1978, we determined that certain issues would be beyond dispute. One of those issues was the authority of the

Scriptures – our faith and practice would be built upon the truths we gleaned from the Scriptures. We believe that God's Word is...

Inspired. His Word is "God-breathed." Therefore, the Bible contains what the Lord wanted said – no more and certainly no less (2 Timothy 3:16).

Immutable. His words abide forever without changing in their appropriateness, relevancy, or certainty (1 Peter 1:25).

Inerrant. God's Word is truth, without any mixture of error, and makes no mistakes (John 17:17).

When we began to outline the principles that would shape our ministry, we looked to the Bible for guidance. Consequently, when we had questions about our ministry as a church, we would ask them in the context of this authoritative source. A church is only equipped for its ministry as it is equipped by the Word of God.

The principles based on the Bible, which I present to you in this book, have helped our congregation define what a church must be in order to bring delight to the heart of God. As we jointly embraced these principles, we joyfully discovered that we gained momentum by moving ahead as one. By capitalizing on biblical unity, we avoided diluting our efforts through the pursuit of different goals.

I challenge you to diligently search the Scriptures and to allow the Word of God to guide you in determining your church's areas of focus and how you approach these ministries. I also advise you not to neglect the Old Testament in your study because it contains many valuable insights on worship (which we will discuss further in Chapters 4-6). Only a thorough examination of the Scriptures for God-given ministry principles will reveal the best possible course to follow if you seek His best for your church.

Let's begin our journey together by examining the roots of a healthy church and by determining what principles and processes described in

God's Word must be followed to establish a church that is firmly "rooted and grounded" (Ephesians 3:17). As the fads and latest ways to "do church" come and go, the church with an established principle-based ministry and a sound foundation in place will continue to faithfully grow for the glory of God. When a church commits itself to the faithful application of biblical principles so that its forms and functions grow out of a well-grounded root system, it will be able to withstand the storms the years will bring.

If the roots of a church are damaged
or inadequate, the days of that church
are numbered.

Continue to live in Him, rooted and

built up in Him, strengthened in the faith.

Colossians 2:6-7 (NIV)

2

Rooted by God's Design

Why would someone travel hundreds of miles to look at a tree? I am referring, of course, to those who flock to see the giant trees in the Sequoia National Park in California. These trees grow to be nearly three hundred feet tall and are supported by huge trunks forty feet in diameter. Their average height is equal to a 25-story building; their base is the width of a city street. They have faced centuries of storms and yet have endured to become awesome and majestic spectacles that draw thousands to see them every year.

Something else about them is also intriguing – although they have relatively shallow root systems compared with their height, their roots intertwine and mingle together for miles underground. As these giant trees grow together in groves, they nourish and uphold each other by their combined strength.

When God calls us to become members of His body, He builds a root system among us to form an interdependent network that grows and produces His kind of fruit. Each church draws its strength from this God-designed root system, and the Church must have vigorous, healthy roots before it can grow and bear the kind of fruit worthy of the One who planted it. If the roots are damaged or inadequate, the days of a tree are numbered. Likewise, if the roots of a church are damaged or inadequate, the days of that church are numbered. Pastors, church leaders, and church members must understand what undergirds the ministry of their church so that they too can be firmly rooted, ready to be built up in Him and established in their faith (Colossians 2:7).

Let's examine together the elements of what God has provided for the Church's vitality and how we can preserve the integrity of the "root system" that supports us in the body of Christ.

The Headship of Jesus Christ

Consider for a moment the tragedy of a young man who became paralyzed in a freak accident – a simple fall backwards in an office chair. Suddenly in one devastating moment, the unexpected blow caused irreversible damage to his spinal cord and left him permanently paralyzed and unable to move from the neck down.

The body can no longer receive signals from the brain when the spinal cord, the pathway of communications from the brain to the body, is injured. The tragedy of paralysis is this: a young, strong athletic body now hangs limp and motionless, no longer able to serve the purpose of its owner.

As it is in the human body, so it is in the Church. Jesus Christ is the Head of the Church, and He wants to direct His Bride to maturity (Colossians 1:18; Ephesians 1:22-23). New Testament writers use a variety of metaphors to describe the Church, but perhaps one of the most helpful terms is "the body of Christ." In Paul's epistles, he chose this term to give better understanding to two concepts, the church's *position* and *function*. When we understand the church's position, we can then better grasp the wonderful opportunity God has given us to fulfill His function.

Everything that happens in the body of Christ must be directed by the Head if we are to serve His purposes. When the body does not receive signals from Christ, the Head of the Church, chaos takes over and the intentions of the Head cannot be satisfactorily accomplished. Each member of the body of Christ must learn to submit to and to take direction from the only true Head, Jesus Christ. Our particular function as members of the body of Christ arises from the direction we receive from Christ. We must constantly try to learn what is pleasing to Him and to commit all that we have and all that we are to expressing our love for Him, by keeping His commandments and doing His will.

The Authority of the Scriptures

With so many ideas and concepts about who God is and what Jesus Christ must be like, the average church member of our generation is hard-pressed to understand just what it is that pleases the Lord. If we do not know what He is like, how can we know what He wants? The answer is surprisingly simple. He has expressed everything we need to know about Him in His Word, the Bible. When I was in college, I came to realize with great relief that since God's Word was true, I could search it fully and at the end of my search I would find Christ, who said "I am...the Truth" (John 14:6). As I examined the truth to my heart's content, I found Jesus Christ through the pages of Scripture (Luke 24:27; Acts 17:11).

God's Word is the standard by which every notion about Him must be measured, and He has made this revelation available to His people in the person of the incarnate Word, Jesus Christ, and in the pages of the inspired Word, the Bible. The revelation of God weighs heavily in His plans for our lives, whether as individuals or as the Church. A holy and perfect God chose to reveal His will in a perfect and faultless way through the pages of an inerrant and infallible Word:

> *"All Scripture is inspired by God and profitable for teaching, for reproof, for correction, for training in righteousness; that the man of God may be adequate, equipped for every good work." (2 Timothy 3:16-17)*

When we base our ministry on biblical principles, we keep the Church on a steady course in accordance with the purposes of God.

The Power of the Holy Spirit

Before Jesus left His disciples and ascended into heaven, He told them to be sure to wait in Jerusalem "until you are clothed with power from on high" (Luke 24:49). He knew that all the knowledge in heaven and earth would be insufficient if the disciples were not endued with the powerful working of the Holy Spirit. In fact, without the Spirit, there is no spiritual life because there has been no spiritual birth: "But if anyone does not have the Spirit of Christ, he does not belong to Him" (Romans 8:9).

Many churches readily embrace the authority of the Scriptures and the headship of Jesus Christ but often fail to rely upon the power of God, which is only available when the Spirit works in the lives of His people. Those who operate from a human base of power are doomed to lifeless forms of religious activity and will never experience what the apostle Peter calls "joy inexpressible" (1 Peter 1:8). This joy is promised to us when the Spirit empowers the individual members of the body to do what the Word says, so that the Head, Jesus Christ, is exalted.

The Oversight of Godly Leaders

Although this resource is categorically different from the other parts of the root system, the role of godly leaders is nonetheless a clear part of God's intention for the life and health of the body of Christ. Within the church, the Lord has always chosen to call godly leaders who function as His servants, the undershepherds of His flock.

Because of their tremendous responsibility, leaders must qualify for leadership and are to be approved only when their lives give evidence of the character traits described in 1 Timothy 3 and Titus 1. Above all else, leaders are to be servants who cannot lead until they have learned to follow Christ. Then the flock can follow, learn from, and even obey these leaders in the church. Paul calls on the flock to "submit to them; for they keep watch over your souls, as those who will give an account" (Hebrews 13:17).

What characteristics should describe godly leaders? This topic will be discussed in more detail later, but here are a few general characteristics:

People of Prayer – whose ministry as servants of the Church is rooted in their dependence upon the Lord and their commitment to pray.

People of Godly Character – who represent Christ in a worthy manner as they hold fast to the truths of God's Word and proclaim, uphold, and defend that Word whatever the cost.

People of Action – who are ready to take bold steps of faith wherever the Lord leads, having counted the cost and considered it worth it all to be found faithful in obeying Christ.

In His infinite wisdom and through His sovereign provision, the Lord God never calls us to do anything for which He does not fully equip us. Together these four fundamental resources – the headship of Jesus Christ, the authority of the Scriptures, the power of the Holy Spirit, and the oversight of godly leaders – form the root system He has designed for every church to be firmly rooted and faithfully growing in Jesus Christ.

Many churches allow the ever-changing preferences of their members to define their way....We need to understand that the Church does not exist for its members.

He is before all things,

and in Him all things hold together.

Colossians 1:17

3

Rooted for God's Purpose

Every summer, our family tries to get away at least once for a few days at the beach. Although I am not a big fan of water sports or of sandy shores, I love the peacefulness that comes when I stand on the shores of something as powerful as the ocean. Watching and listening as the waves pound the sand, I find that I am relaxed and feel safe and secure because I belong to the God who controls the waves!

Somehow all of this helps me put things in perspective. For as long as the earth has existed, the waves have pounded those shores and long after I am gone, they will continue to do so. In the context of this history, I am compelled to ask myself what I am doing during my stay here in this world. What is my purpose here? Am I living according to the priorities that will accomplish that purpose?

As a church, we must ask ourselves the same questions: Why are we here? What is our purpose here? What is God's purpose for us? Churches are placed in danger when members become so preoccupied with themselves that they lose sight of God. Many churches allow the ever-changing preferences of their members to define their way, rather than looking to Christ to be the Way. We need to understand that the Church does not exist for its members. Our focus must return to the place where it should be – on Christ.

We cannot afford to neglect all that Christ has called us to be and do by diverting our energy and attention to lesser things, personal interests, or vain pursuits. Paul's challenge needs repeating in every church regularly so that our focus is kept fixed on what is best:

> *"If then you have been raised up with Christ, keep seeking the things above, where Christ is, seated at the right hand of God. Set your mind on the things above, not on the things that are on earth." (Colossians 3:1-2)*

Generations of believers have expressed the purpose of life in a concise answer given to the first question asked in the Westminster Catechism, "What is the chief end of man?" The correct response is "To glorify God and enjoy Him forever." So it must be for the Church, since it is composed of those who embrace that holy purpose both individually and collectively.

Yet how are we as the Church supposed to glorify God? The answer to that question compelled us to do two things early in our ministry at Providence.

First, we had to explore the principles upon which the ministry of the Church is based, so we conducted an extensive biblical study of the goals and purposes of the Bride of Christ. Working through the Bible, we found all the principles necessary for our church to operate in a biblically sound manner. We followed this simple method:

1. **Observation.** What do the texts say?

2. **Interpretation.** What do they mean? What principles do we find?

3. **Application.** How do they apply in our situation?

Second, we had to find out *what* we were supposed to do (the biblical content of the ministry) and *how* we were supposed to do it (the godly character of the ministry).

The first thing we discovered was that the early church glorified God by leading people to know Jesus Christ as Savior and then building them up to maturity in Him. For many years, we expressed this focus in terms of a twofold emphasis in our ministry, evangelism and edification, but later we realized worship (exaltation) was missing as an important component. Here is our statement of purpose:

> Providence Baptist Church exists in order that we may glorify the Lord through the biblical means of exaltation, leading each other to worship Him in spirit and truth; evangelism, introducing people to Jesus Christ; and edification, building each other up to maturity in Him.

Through this book, we will work through each of these areas by highlighting the governing principles that give shape and substance to each one. In order to develop the godly character of the ministry, we have to identify those principles that best personify the character of Christ and demonstrate the traits most consistent with what pleases Christ.

Before we explore what we should be doing, I would like to share an experience I had as a new pastor. I was asked to participate in a meeting of leaders from a local congregation, and their objective was to put together the calendar of ministry events for the coming year. Since they had obviously done this many times and I was new to the process, I was unclear about the criteria being used to decide what made it and what was cut.

From my perspective, there did not seem to be any controlling set of priorities or stated objectives by which they were being asked to determine what to do. Eventually, being young and not knowing any better, I asked if there was any particular goal toward which they were aiming or any purpose for doing some of the things scheduled for the coming year. The strange looks directed my way let me know in no uncertain terms that asking questions was out of order, unnecessary, and would simply prolong the progress they were making.

I soon realized that I was witnessing what many churches do as a matter of course. They were putting plans in place to "do church" the way it had been done for years. They never paused to ask if what they were doing was actually working toward anything substantial to accomplish God's will or making a difference in the lives of the people to whom they were ministering. In order to get down to the content of the ministry, or what they were going to do, they had skipped the essential steps of determining their overall purpose and reviewing the foundations of their root system.

I mention this experience as a word of caution. If we begin with what to do rather than why we must do it, we resign ourselves to unfulfilling and ineffective labors that will bear no lasting fruit. If we don't understand why we are doing what we do, then doing anything at all seems to have enough value in itself. Perhaps this helps explain the busy but unfruitful ministries of so many churches. Therefore, when we discuss the content of ministry, we can never allow anything to sever the connection between the why, the what, and the how of our labors together.

Why are we supposed to worship? What is effective evangelism supposed to look like? How will we know that we have done what we should to build up people in Christ, to edify them? We are to search the Scriptures, observe what the church of the New Testament did, sort out the principles behind what was done, and then figure out how those principles apply in our church today. This process will provide the direction needed to determine what we should do and what the content of our ministry should be.

Regardless of the approach we take, if we are not keenly aware that apart from Christ we can do nothing, we will amount to nothing. The greatest testimony that can be made about a church is that the Lord is there, making His presence known in a mighty and majestic way among His people. God is there...

- Revealing His glory and filling us with awe

- Touching lives with His comfort and peace

- Reaching out to desperate and heartbroken sinners with the redeeming forgiveness and love of Christ

- Mending wounded marriages and healing broken homes

- Challenging His "salty and shining" people to confront the evils of a fallen world

- Answering prayers and burdening our hearts to be faithful intercessors

- Moving among His people and empowering lives of obedience

People may come to a church because of its beautiful music, dynamic programs for children and youth, doctrinal soundness, its preaching and teaching ministry, and a host of other reasons. However, if they are looking to know God, they will not stay if they do not learn and see more of Christ. Our future as a church depends upon our commitment to keep Christ at the center of all that we do and make Him the focus of everything we do.

Section Two

THE BIBLICAL CONTENT OF MINISTRY

Whatever you do in word or deed,
do all in the name of the Lord.
Colossians 3:17

The worship that takes place around the throne of God, as described in the Bible, would almost certainly be viewed with disdain by many modern worshipers.

God is spirit, and those who worship Him

must worship in spirit and truth.

John 4:24

4

Defining Biblical Worship

Can there be any topic more worthy of our consideration than worship of the sovereign God? Of the three major areas that determine the content of what we do as a church – worship, evangelism, and edification – only worship will continue forever. The day will come when we will no longer evangelize because the day of salvation will pass, and the Savior will return for His people to take them to be with Him forever. After that day, judgment will come and no more invitations to come to salvation through Jesus Christ will be extended. Likewise, when we go to be with Him, the means by which we grow to maturity will not be needed since the Bible tells us that when we see Him we shall be made like Him and shall be complete in Him (1 John 3:2; Colossians 1:28).

Worship, however, will be our joy through all eternity. We will never cease to praise and exalt Him as the One to whom all glory is due forever and ever. Therefore, one of the most exhilarating exercises possible is discovering what God Himself desires when He seeks those who want to worship Him. In other words, don't settle for just shuffling through familiar routines of "church worship services," for Jesus said,

> *"An hour is coming, and now is, when the true worshipers shall worship the Father in spirit and truth; for such people the Father seeks to be His worshipers. God is spirit and those who worship Him must worship in spirit and truth."*
> *(John 4:23-24)*

The very idea that God is looking for people to be His worshipers should both excite and challenge us. We should be thrilled that He is seeking such people and should determine that by His grace we will be among those He finds. Yet we should also be challenged to go beyond our own limited ideas and the small frames we use to picture what worship really is. Something as glorious and majestic as worship needs to be explored as fervently as we would seek after rich veins of precious gold. When we limit our search to the surface of our own experiences and the scope of our own traditions, we risk missing the fullness of this treasured calling. What help do we find in the descriptions of and prescriptions for worship in the Scriptures?

Trying to summarize the Bible's extensive treatment of worship in one chapter presents a challenge beyond my ability. Nothing I can say will be sufficient to express all that needs to be said about this lofty subject, but perhaps this limited attempt will capture in some small way the magnitude of our calling to be the people God is seeking to worship Him. I cringe when I hear people dismiss one style or another as "not worshipful" or as "offensive," choosing to sit in judgment of the value of worship experiences unlike their own. The worship that takes place around the throne of God, as described in the Bible (Revelation 7:9-12), would almost certainly be viewed with disdain by many modern worshipers who have appointed themselves as authorities on what God will and will not accept. These "authorities" ignore the fact that God presents a vast diversity of worship approaches in His Word that all meet with His approval.

The principles of worship offer tremendous flexibility and freedom in how we actually approach the Lord in worship, what we do when we worship, and how we are transformed by the experience. Therefore, I find great joy in considering these different principles of worship, knowing full well that they are but a hint of what the Lord really has in store for those who would seek Him in adoring praise and with overflowing gratitude.

Worship Must Be Christ-centered

Worship is the immediate response of the person who comes into the presence of the Lord God Almighty. To see Him and understand that He is God, to approach Him and acknowledge that He is holy and glorious, demands that we bow down in humble, reverent awe and worship Him.

Until we know Christ and His saving grace, we cannot come before the Lord since our sin forbids it. We are totally separated from Him and have no right nor means of going to Him until that sin has been forgiven and the stain of it washed away.

The Old Testament is filled with instructions and provisions for the worship of the Lord, but in every case the basis of true worship is worthiness, something inherent in no one but God Himself (see Revelation 5:1-14). Therefore, every principle of worship found in the Scriptures speaks of the preparation of those who come to worship so that they might be made worthy. That is why every form of instruction, every example of adoration and praise, focuses on the one and only Mediator between God and man, the Lord Jesus Christ. Worship must be centered on Christ, who makes us worthy, or it is not true worship.

Worship Must Be Consecrated

Worship originates with God Himself. The very idea of worship begins with the acknowledgement that human existence relies on the existence of One who is greater, One who deserves our worship. All that we know about Him depends on what He has revealed to us about Himself. Therefore, our worship begins with and focuses on His revelation of Himself. Worship itself is a consecration of ourselves to God, a holy response to what He has made known. What does the Bible say about what He has revealed about Himself?

True Worship Reveals His Glory

The Bible is filled with accounts of God's revelation of His glory. From the heavens declaring His glory (Psalm 19:1) to Moses' vision of the glory of God passing by as he hid in the cleft of the rock (Exodus 33:18-23) to the Word becoming flesh and dwelling among us that we might behold His glory (John 1:14), God offers glimpses of something so magnificent that those who see it fall down and tremble.

The prophet Ezekiel wrote of his glimpse of the glory of God: "As the appearance of the rainbow in the clouds on a rainy day, so was the appearance of the surrounding radiance. Such was the appearance of the likeness of the glory of the Lord. And when I saw it, **I fell on my face**" (Ezekiel 1:28). True worship begins when we grasp something of the nature of the glory of God and then bow before Him in awestruck reverence.

True Worship Reveals His Perfect Worthiness

Once we understand who He is, an understanding granted to us by His grace, we see that He alone is worthy to receive worship. No one else compares with Him and that realization alone compels us to turn away from every unworthy object of our affections and devote our hearts to Him alone. His worthiness generates a desire to worship Him and declare with those gathered around the throne in the book of Revelation, "Worthy art Thou, our Lord and our God, to receive glory and honor and power; for Thou didst create all things, and because of Thy will they existed, and were created" (Revelation 4:11).

True Worship Reveals His Dominion

As the one and only God, unique in every possible way, He also has dominion, authority, and power over all things. He is Lord of all: "And to Him was given dominion, glory and a kingdom, that all the peoples, nations, and men of every language might serve Him. His dominion is an everlasting dominion which will not pass away; and His kingdom is one which will not be destroyed" (Daniel 7:14). When God spoke to the Israelites through Moses and Aaron, He emphasized that dominion and the response He expects to this revelation of His character: "Consecrate yourselves therefore, and be holy; for I am holy" (Leviticus 11:44).

Our response to the revelation of God's glory, dominion, and perfect worthiness can be no less than consecrated worship, or worship that has been made worthy by the grace of Jesus Christ at work in us to cleanse us from unrighteousness and make us holy. Otherwise, how would we dare to approach such an awesome God?

Worship Must Be Confessional

The Greek word for the verb "confess" is *homologeo,* which translated literally means "to say the same thing." In our worship, we are called to say the same things that God says, to believe what He believes, to hate what He hates, and to love what He loves. Elements within our worship experience need to speak confessionally to the Lord. Confessional elements often get lost in much of the contemporary worship of modern churches.[1] Scriptural worship always includes confession as part of the proper response of a believing heart to a holy God.

We Must Confess Sin with Contrition

Since God is perfect in holiness, nothing less than holy worship can be acceptable to Him. Consequently, we cannot approach Him with confidence that we will be welcome in His presence unless our sin has been forgiven and our unrighteousness cleared away. Just as Isaiah responded by crying out, "Woe is me, for I am ruined! Because I am a man of unclean lips, and I live among a people of unclean lips; for my eyes have seen the King, the Lord of hosts" (Isaiah 6:5), each person daring to come before the Lord needs to realize the depth of our alienation from Him. When we see

---

1 By contemporary worship, I am not referring to a worship style but to worship that is current in the culture of our day. Traditional, blended, contemporary, and alternative worship styles all tend to suffer from a lack of consistent practices of confession as a regular part of the order of worship. Liturgical churches tend to do better with this important component than those with less-structured forms, but they sometimes do so without feeling or passion, resorting to what Isaiah referred to when he wrote, "Then the Lord said, Because [the] people draw near with their words and honor Me with their lip service...and their reverence for Me consists of tradition learned by rote" (Isaiah 29:13).

our sin as God does, we will confess it to Him with broken and contrite hearts and call out for His forgiveness. Our worship depends upon the purity and holiness of our hearts. Therefore, we must come to worship with our sin confessed and enter His presence in a manner worthy of those who belong to Christ.

We Must Confess Christ in Faith

Our salvation depends entirely upon the grace of God in Jesus Christ: "If you confess with your mouth Jesus as Lord, and believe in your heart that God raised Him from the dead, you shall be saved" (Romans 10:9). By confessing faith in His name, we are granted access to "draw near with confidence to the throne of grace" so that in Him our worship might be pleasing to the Father (Hebrews 4:16). Coming in His name, confessing faith in Him, we enter worship as those who no longer rely on our own vain efforts to gain His favor, but acknowledge that He alone can bring us near to the Lord.

We Must Confess Truth in Doctrine

Jesus said that worship should be in spirit and truth (John 4:23-24). Without confessing the truth and agreeing with the sound doctrine of God's Word, how could we hope to offer our worship to the One we have offended by abandoning His truth? The deceptions and false ideas so highly acclaimed by those who refuse the revealed truth of God find an audience only among unbelievers in a fallen world. They have no place before the Lord nor do those who espouse them.

God must be worshiped as He truly is by those who believe rightly about Him and confess their genuine hope in the authenticity of the "faith which was once for all delivered to the saints" (Jude 3b). Creating alternate versions of reality based on our own imaginations may appeal to some, but not to those who understand that the entertainment of ideas that falsely describe God amounts to nothing more than idolatry.[2] To worship God in

---

2 A. W. Tozer, *The Knowledge of the Holy* (New York: Harper & Row, 1975).

truth, we must believe what He has said about Himself and confess our confidence in the sound doctrines of biblical theology.

Worship that is confessional is anchored in the eternal truth about God and about ourselves in relationship to Him. Our worship must say the same thing in harmonious agreement with what He would say. Jesus prayed, "Sanctify them in the truth; Thy word is truth" (John 17:17). For our worship to be sanctified, it must flow from His truth and be confessed with our lips.

Worship Must Be Celebrative

Freedom brings celebration! When Christ set us free from sin by His redeeming grace and released us from hopelessness by revealing the mercies of the Father, He gave us every reason to rejoice. Somehow many churches have lost the sense of celebration in their worship and have allowed it to degenerate into the deadly ritual of a religious ceremony that has been stripped of any signs of life. Reading through the accounts of worship in the Bible leads me to conclude that we have missed something if we deprive ourselves of vibrant expressions of praise in worship.

Celebrating with Songs of Joy

Beyond just the descriptions of joyful celebrations in the Old Testament and the instructions of the Psalms to sing new songs of joy to the Lord, the New Testament also describes how worship is to be filled with the music of the heart. When our hearts have been stirred by the Lord's power and mercy and our lives transformed by His abiding presence, the response will be songs of joyful praise.

Paul said that when the "Word richly dwells within you" and you are "filled with the Spirit," the overflow will produce "psalms and hymns and spiritual songs," and you will inevitably find yourself "making melody with your heart to the Lord" and "singing with thankfulness in your hearts to

God."[3] How our worship would be transformed if more believers took these matters to heart! As it is, some do not think that any song is "worshipful" unless it conforms to musical styles of previous centuries and does not express itself with too much enthusiasm.

As I read through the Scriptures, I cannot help but see that God obviously loves music and delights in this aspect of our worship. Note the words of Zephaniah: "The Lord your God is with you, He is mighty to save. He will take great delight in you, He will quiet you with His love, He will rejoice over you **with singing**" (Zephaniah 3:17 NIV). God Himself expresses His delight in song, so how can we not do so as well?

Celebrating with Expressions of Delight

Once we realize that celebration in worship mirrors the actual delight within God's own heart, we begin to see why it pleases Him greatly to receive a variety of "expressions of delight" from His people. Scripture records that when His people are excited by His presence and filled with His joy they erupt with many forms of expressive behavior:

> *Shouts of Joy.* "Shout joyfully to God, all the earth; sing the glory of His name; make His praise glorious" (Psalm 66:1; see also Psalm 81:1; 95:1-2, 98:4, and 100:1). When I was growing up, some of the older, more demonstrative men would punctuate the worship with shouts of "Amen, Hallelujah!" as they affirmed what was being said or sung. Today those shouts might take a different form, use different words, come from different age groups, but there is still a place for shouts of joy in worship. Granted, there are some who will abuse this, as they will any legitimate expression of worship, but the abusers should not be allowed to nullify the voices of genuine praise among us.

---

3 Ephesians 5:18-19 and Colossians 3:16 deserve careful thought. Both speak of a level of spiritual maturity in worship and growth that needs to be practiced more faithfully. Usually the focus stops with the exhortations to "be filled with the Spirit" and to "let the Word of Christ richly dwell within you" without reading further to see what God expects to happen next. The fullness of Christ results in the music of the heart!

Instrumental Praise. "Sing praises to the Lord with the lyre; with the lyre and the sound of melody. With trumpets and the sound of the horn shout joyfully before the King, the Lord" (Psalm 98:5-6). After several centuries of worship services accompanied only by piano or organ, Western churches are becoming reacquainted with the biblical practice of using many different instruments in public worship.

New Songs. "Give thanks to the Lord with the lyre; sing praises to Him with a harp of ten strings. Sing to Him a new song; play skillfully with a shout of joy" (Psalm 33:2-3). Each generation needs to invest their best efforts in developing new worship songs that express the ideas of their minds and the feelings of their hearts. Care needs to be taken not to dismiss or forsake the work of previous generations; however, new songs that are biblically sound and musically able to integrate lyrics and melody in a meaningful way should always be welcome in the Church.

Raised Hands. "So I will bless Thee as long as I live; I will lift up my hands in Thy name" (Psalm 63:4). Paul wrote, "Therefore, I want the men in every place to pray, lifting up holy hands, without wrath and dissension" (1 Timothy 2:8). Unfortunately, the practice of raising hands as an expression of worship became associated almost exclusively with charismatic and Pentecostal styles of worship over the last twenty-five years of the twentieth century. Many believers who differed theologically with charismatic doctrine avoided outwardly expressive worship patterns because they were afraid that others might think that they embraced not only their worship practices but also their theology.

Although I do not find that I am inclined to lift my hands when I worship, many others do and should enjoy their freedom to do so since they are clearly in-line with a biblical means of expression. However, those who prefer not to lift their hands should be afforded the same freedom as those who want the freedom to raise their hands.

Clapping. "O clap your hands, all peoples; shout to God with the voice of joy" (Psalm 47:1). Yes, it is true. Clapping is a legitimate form of worshipful expression. Whether clapping occurs as a response to something that has generated a desire to express appreciation, like a moving testimony or a stirring song, or if it occurs as a rhythmic participation in the worship music that accompanies the singing, we find that clapping was not viewed with disapproving attitudes or accused of being irreverent in the Psalms. In some ways, clapping has taken the place of shouts of joy as a means of expressing affirmation and appreciation during times of corporate worship.

Dancing with Joy. "And Miriam the prophetess, Aaron's sister, took the timbrel in her hand, and all the women went out after her with timbrels and dancing" (Exodus 15:20). We also read in 2 Samuel 6:14-15: "And David was dancing before the Lord with all his might, and David was wearing a linen ephod. So David and all the house of Israel were bringing up the ark of the Lord with shouting and the sound of the trumpet." For those from the regulative school of worship who restrict corporate worship only to those practices described in the New Testament, dance would never be allowed as a part of worship. However, the presence of dancing as a legitimate means of celebration in the Old Testament cannot be denied.

Choirs. "Then I had the leaders of Judah come up on top of the wall, and I appointed two great choirs, the first proceeding to the right on top of the wall...the second choir proceeded to the left...and the singers sang, with Jezrahiah their leader, and on that day they offered great sacrifices and rejoiced because God had given them great joy, even the women and children rejoiced, so that the joy of Jerusalem was heard from afar" (Nehemiah 12:31, 38, 42-43). For those who think of choirs as performing troops who put on a show and should not play a role in worship, the Old Testament accounts of their place in leading worship should prompt them to reconsider whether their objections are based on personal preference or biblical conviction.

Drawing from the wealth of biblical examples of worship, we can conclude rather easily that celebration played a large role in the practices of worship found throughout the Scriptures. The basis of this celebrative attitude is the relationship God has called us to enjoy with Him through His Son Jesus Christ.

Worship Must Be Contemplative

While reading through the previous discussion of celebrative worship, some of you probably became uncomfortable because you believe that worship should only be contemplative. Yet the Scriptures reveal that worship should be contemplative, but not in a way that excludes the celebrative aspects of worship. Celebration and contemplation are complementary partners in genuine worship. Celebration can be noisy and sometimes may seem on the verge of being out of control, but contemplation calls for a turn toward stillness and quietness. Accommodating both in the same worship time can be difficult, but part of the beauty of God's design is that even the impossible becomes possible. We can enjoy both the inexpressible joy of our relationship with Jesus Christ and retreat into reflective awe out of reverence for our sovereign God. Biblical worship expects us to pursue them both and find the wonder of the Lord in either.

Contemplating with Reflection

A. W. Tozer wrote that most modern worshipers have "lost [their] spirit of worship and ability to withdraw inwardly to meet God in adoring silence."[4] In contrast to today's expectation of instantaneous access to whatever we want, when we approach the Lord to worship Him, there can be no hurry. We cannot rush God! The Lord Himself says to us, "Be still and

---

4 A. W. Tozer, *The Knowledge of the Holy* (New York: Harper & Row, 1975) 6.

know that I am God" (Psalm 46:10 KJV). In our haste, many valuable worship opportunities have been squandered because we refuse to be still, to be quiet, and to listen. Ample time must be given for meditation, or we may miss Him entirely even though He was present and waiting to meet us.

We need time to think about who He really is, reflect on what He has done by His grace, consider the relationship between the attributes and actions of God, ponder the impact His power should have on the way we trust Him, meditate on His Word, and allow our finite minds to trace the course of His infinite mercy as far as we can. Most of the time, corporate worship cannot offer the extensive amount of time we need for pure reflection. We must set aside personal worship times for more intimate sessions of reflection when we are alone with God. Still, we need to provide some time for reflection whenever the Church gathers to worship.

Contemplating with Humbleness

Contemplation frequently transports us from the peaks of celebration to the valleys and plains of humbleness. Just as our relationship with Christ makes our hearts leap for joy, our reverence for Him takes us to our knees as we bow down before Him. His awesome splendor serves to highlight the shadowy darkness of our human nature. Therefore, humility will always accompany honest worship. We kneel before Him because we see Him as He is and only then realize who we really are, the unworthy recipients of mercy and grateful beneficiaries of grace. Approaching worship with a boastful and prideful spirit completely destroys any chance to enter into the presence of the Lord. The psalmist wrote, "A broken and a contrite heart, O God, Thou wilt not despise" (Psalm 51:17b).

Contemplation of the holiness and majesty and glory of God will always produce humility so that our worship maintains an air of gentle dignity and respect for who He is. Even in the liveliest moments of celebration, the element of humility in our worship prevents it from dissolving into a disorderly display of ostentatious behavior.

Contemplating with Affection

In quiet moments of contemplation, we meet Christ in such a way that He confides in us and shares the depth of His love for us. I once heard it said that God is not the kind of Lover who shouts His affections across the crowded marketplace, but reserves His intimate expressions of love for those moments when we can be still and know that He is God. There in the quiet place we also learn to declare our love for Him and devote our hearts to Him. Announcing our love from the heights of celebrative praise is exhilarating, but our affection moves to another level when we learn how to affirm that love in the sweet moments of quietness to which He calls each of us.

Henry Scougal,[5] a seventeenth-century pastor/author, challenged my heart when he wrote these words describing the love of God:

> "The love of God is a delightful and affectionate sense of the Divine perfections, which makes the soul resign and sacrifice itself wholly unto Him, desiring above all things to please Him, and delighting in nothing so much as in fellowship and communion with Him, and being ready to do or suffer any thing for His sake, or at His pleasure."

Contemplative worship begins with a deep sense of reverence for God, awed by His majestic splendor but then transformed by His amazing grace and abounding love.

Worship Must Be Comprehensive

Biblical worship refuses to be confined to a single category. It is too comprehensive to accept the limitations of being nothing more than an occasional religious duty. Churches do a grave disservice to their members when the word "worship" only describes the weekly expressions of corporate praise. When God calls us to worship, He calls us to a

5 Henry Scougal, *The Life of God in the Soul of Man* (Great Britain: Christian Focus Publications, 1996) 10.

comprehensive engagement of all that we are in order to glorify and honor Him for all that He is in Christ Jesus. The fact that He abides in us, calls us the temple of the Holy Spirit, and refers to us as His sanctuary should clue us in to the magnitude of His design for the worship He seeks from His people.

True Worship is a Life-encompassing Commitment

What part of your life should be exempt from worship? Paul wrote, "Whatever you do in word or deed, do all in the name of the Lord Jesus, giving thanks through Him to God the Father...do all to the glory of God" (Colossians 3:17; 1 Corinthians 10:31).

When you accepted the life Christ gave you, the terms of that gift were never hidden or presented in a way that represented anything less than full disclosure. You belong to Him and all that you are has been set apart for His glory. Worship flows naturally from heart, mind, and soul when you understand that even your body has been designated as a worship center for His praise. You are called "to present your bodies a living and holy sacrifice, acceptable to God, which is your spiritual service of worship" (Romans 12:1). Wherever you take your body, you cannot escape the fact that you are in the service of worship right where you are, doing whatever you are doing.

Living a life of unceasing worship also establishes two other dimensions that expand your influence as a servant of Jesus Christ. With Him as the central focus of your life, you cannot help but have an impact in both an *evangelistic* and an *ethical* way. When your life constantly exalts Christ, the people around you are forced to deal with an authentic encounter with the Lord. Jesus said, "If I be lifted up from the earth, I will draw all men to Myself" (John 12:32). The daily commitment you make to lift Him up will draw others to Christ by presenting Him in such a compelling way that they will be drawn through your witness of worship to Him.

The impact on our ethics is also significant. No one can survive a divided heart. If you try to worship with genuineness while harboring grudges against others, discriminating against another person, or persisting in unethical or immoral behavior, God makes it clear in His Word that you are wasting your time. As the psalmist said, "If I regard wickedness in my heart, the Lord will not hear" (Psalm 66:18).

Jesus addressed the issue from another perspective when He said:

> *"If therefore you are presenting your offering at the altar, and there remember that your brother has something against you, leave your offering there before the altar, and go your way; first be reconciled to your brother, and then come and present your offering." (Matthew 5:23-24)*

The ethical dimension of worship seldom receives the attention it deserves. Consequently, much of our worship in the modern church era suffers irreparable damage because our hearts are not in order before the Lord when we come to worship Him. Worship comprehensively impacts every area of our lives. With nothing withheld, we freely offer Him all that we are in a life-encompassing commitment to glorify Him in everything.

True Worship Brings a Life-changing Perspective

This commitment that encompasses our entire lives results in a life-changing perspective. We finally recognize that our eternal occupation, which we formerly believed was in heaven only, has already begun. We begin to realize that our reason for living is to bring glory to God in whatever we do and that our entire life is our "spiritual service of worship" (Romans 12:1).

When the body of Christ comes together for worship – as we must to honor God's design – we owe it to Him to come only with the desire for Christ to be exalted. As we lay aside the encumbrances of our personal preferences and expectations, we should find delight in every phase of corporate worship. But that will happen only when our perspective changes from a self-focused view of what "meets my needs" to a Christ-focused desire to honor the One to whom we owe everything.

The things that delight the heart of our heavenly Father must delight us as well. Worship at its deepest level is abiding in the presence of God and glorifying Him for all that He is to us through Christ Jesus His Son.

A one-dimensional approach to worship
reduces it, trivializes it, and marginalizes it to
the extent that it has little impact on us and
little value to God.

Come, let us worship and bow down,

let us kneel before the Lord our Maker.

Psalm 95:6

5

Developing a Life of Worship

Can there be another subject that we are so familiar with and yet know so little about? Almost all of us have an opinion on what true worship is, what kinds of worship we like, and more likely, what kinds of worship we do *not* like. Still, I would be willing to guess that fewer than one-fourth of the believers I know get beyond the mental image of a "corporate gathering" when they think about worship.

Worship is so closely connected in our minds with an event that takes place at a designated building called a "church," at a certain time and day of the week, and with a specific format and carefully crafted order that any further image is hard to visualize.

Yet worship must be far more than a weekly event if the Church is to succeed in bringing glory to God. There are at least three kinds of worship found in God's Word and practiced among His people: personal worship, family worship, and corporate worship. For the Church to meet His expectations for worship, the level of our expectations for every member needs to rise to meet these biblical standards.

Personal Worship

Due to well-intended efforts of worship leaders to generate an "atmosphere" conducive to true worship, many who attend meetings for corporate worship become nothing more than spectators. Rather than having the inward testimony of the Spirit born out of genuine times of refreshment in the presence of the Lord alone, these spectators rely on what someone else does to make worship happen. Eventually they become self-styled "theater critics," who assess success or failure by the subjective standards of their own tastes.

The idea of meeting the Lord alongside others in adoring praise seldom occurs to those who have not learned to meet the Lord when they are alone. Church members play a major role in the character of corporate worship by the way they prepare for it on their own. Each of us is responsible for arranging our lives so that a portion of each day is set aside to meet with God. We must have time to do more than just casually read a devotional gem or a familiar portion of Scripture. We need the opportunity to allow the truths we have discovered about the Lord to ascend to the One who is worthy to be praised in personal expressions of worship.

Although this is not the place to go into the logistics of how to develop a personal time of worship, I would strongly encourage you to pursue this lofty goal as one that will continue to challenge you for the rest of your life. As you develop your own practical plan to meet daily with the Lord, you must make provision for each of the following:

Consistent Worship

Although the demands of life and even ministry can be relentless, lack of personal discipline in many of our lives makes consistency a daunting challenge for us. Yet we need the constant presence of spiritual nurture in our daily lives even more than we need physical food. Our time with the Lord in personal worship must be consistent.

Reverent Worship

Never allow the fact that He is the sovereign Lord to drift from your thinking when you approach Him. Certainly, He desires personal fellowship with you but that never means that He is less than the same holy God whose glory may not be seen by the eye of sinful man! Reverence is always appropriate before the Lord.

Intimate Worship

How do we balance reverence with intimacy? Only the Lord can bring the two together, something He has done perfectly through Christ. What an amazing privilege to be granted intimate access to the heart of the Creator of all things! Make sure that you pursue the personal side of God so that your worship does not degenerate into a ritual maintained at a cool distance, where your head and not your heart is engaged in worship.

Meditative Worship

Haste and efficiency have their positive points, but not in personal worship. Rushing through our time alone with the Lord keeps us from quiet listening and reflecting upon God Himself. Worship without meditation cannot help but fail. Therefore, in your plans for personal worship, allow for enough time to meditate and reflect on the Lord and all that He longs to show you.

When our concept of worship diminishes to the point that only corporate worship remains, we cannot hope to find the richness and depth that God intends for us in His plan for worship. A one-dimensional approach to worship reduces it, trivializes it, and marginalizes it to the extent that it has little impact on us and little value to God. The substance of public worship arises from substantive, meaningful times of personal worship.

Family Worship

After declining to near extinction, family worship has experienced a resurgence in recent years. Few areas have been as difficult for me personally than maintaining any degree of consistency in leading family times of worship. Yet I know that without accepting that responsibility and building a firm foundation in the home, all that happens in public or corporate worship is likely to remain an empty shell.

Churches cannot provide what families neglect. Many homes look to their churches to take care of all the biblical instruction, discipleship, training, and ministry involvement for their family members and are quick to assign blame when the institution called the church does not "meet their needs." It is true that the body of Christ should function as an equipping center and worshiping center to support and encourage members in fulfilling their familial spiritual duties. Yet in the Scriptures, the main responsibility for such things rests primarily upon the family. The Lord instructs us to impress the things of God upon the hearts of each member of our family:

> *"These commandments that I give you today are to be upon your hearts. Impress them on your children. Talk about them when you sit at home and when you walk along the road, when you lie down and when you get up. Tie them as symbols on your hands and bind them on your foreheads."* (Deuteronomy 6:6-8 NIV)

Now that our sons have grown older and are establishing homes of their own, I want to remember our times at home together with special fondness. I want to remember with gladness and not regret our times of family devotions, our decisions made together based on biblical principles, and even our times of discipline anchored in the character and the content of God's Word. We enjoyed wonderful successes in many ways and in others, disappointing failures. If I could offer godly counsel to young mothers and fathers, it would be to keep your lives simple enough to maintain regular times with the family for fellowship and encouragement in the Lord.

When seventeenth-century pastor Richard Baxter wrote *The Reformed Pastor*,[1] one of his points of emphasis was family worship. He believed

---

1 Richard Baxter, *The Reformed Pastor* (abridged) (Portland, Oregon: Multonomah Press, 1982) 79-80.

pastors were not fulfilling their calling if they allowed the families of their congregations to neglect worshiping together in their homes:

> "We must also have a special care for families to see that they are well-ordered and that each performs its duties. For the life of religion, and the welfare and glory of the church and state, depend much on family government and duty. If we neglect this we will undo all. How can we see to the revival of a whole congregation if all the work is cast upon the pastor alone? Or if the heads of families neglect their responsibilities, what will be the extent of a church awakening?
>
> "If any good is begun by the pastoral ministry, it will be stopped – or at least hindered – if the family is careless, prayerless, and worldly. But if you get the heads of families to do their part, to take up the work where you have left off, and then finally to help it on, what an abundance of good might be done! So I urge you to see the importance of family cooperation in your ministry.
>
> "Your goal is to be effective in family ministry. So get information about how each family is organized, and how God is worshiped there. Visit the families when they are at leisure and find out if the head of the family prays within his home, reads the Scriptures, enters into worship in other ways. Labor to convince those who are negligent about the validity of such duties; ask that they promise to reform their ways for the future."

Nearly a century later in Colonial America, a Presbyterian pastor named Samuel Davies[2] wrote similar sentiments in a letter to the heads of households in his congregation:

> "Were your families made for this world or the next? If for the next, then religion must be maintained in them, for

---

2 Samuel Davies, *The Godly Family,* 2nd ed. (Morgan, Pennsylvania: Soli Deo Gloria Publications, 1996) 12-15.

that alone can prepare you for eternity...must not religion be maintained in your families? They should be nurseries for heaven, and that they cannot be if you banish devotion from them....How can you expect that your children and your servants will become worshipers of the God of heaven if they have been educated in the neglect of family religion? Can prayerless parents expect to have praying children? If you neglect to instruct them, can you expect they will grow up in the knowledge of God and of themselves....Their souls, sirs, their immortal souls, are entrusted to your care, and you must give a solemn account of your trust....I beseech, I entreat, I charge you to begin and continue the worship of God in your families from this day to the close of your lives."

Family worship feeds the fires of corporate worship by training and teaching and practicing the elements of worship in the secure environment of the home – where questions can be asked, skills in singing developed, the language of thanksgiving and praise learned, and an expectant atmosphere cultivated. We must not deprive ourselves or the next generation of this rich treasure.

Corporate Worship

When the people of God come together for times of corporate worship, a sense of celebration and rejoicing often prevails because we have come to meet the Lord. If there is no sense of expectation, no sense of personal preparation, no context of personal or family worship, we cannot count on anything more than just another public meeting. Yet when we are ready and willing, when our hearts are focused on Christ, when the biblical character of worship is respected and observed, each new time of corporate worship has the potential to be a memorable meeting with the Lord.

The "spectator mentality" easily creeps into the experience of many churches when the time comes for meeting together for corporate worship. When a large group gathers for worship, every person should be a participant, not just a witness. Granted, the size of the crowd can create a climate that allows anonymity, but true worship should include all present as we approach the throne of God's grace collectively to offer our worship in the name of His Son, Jesus Christ.

Whether you are the worship leader in front of the congregation, or the one who takes the last seat in the back of the room, you must recognize that in worship there is an audience of only One. What takes place in true worship is intended to honor only the Lord and is offered to Him for His approval and pleasure. We pervert the very intent of worship when we approach it with an attitude that focuses on "getting something out of it," rather than giving all that we are to Him alone.

I can learn to tolerate many styles of worship, a tremendous diversity of music, a wide range of preaching techniques, differences in orders of worship, even make allowances for the inconveniences of the room or building in which the meeting takes place, if my heart is set on exalting the Lord with wholehearted, adoring worship!

Today at the beginning of the twenty-first century, the tides of change seem to be at work in public worship as the old and new styles each have advocates and detractors. As some churches cling to the forms which have been defined over the past two to three hundred years in Protestant churches, others have totally forsaken them, choosing instead to substitute more familiar styles of music and methods of communicating eternal truths. Many churches have sought to blend the best of the old and new together and recognize that content rather than style matters most to the One to whom our worship is given. Change in the outward expressions of worship will not matter so much if the inward desires remain fixed on meeting the Lord in adoring praise and worship.

Seeking God's Delight

Our chief concern in worship always must be God's delight. Will my worship bring delight to the heart of God? Are others finding joy in authentic worship even if it is not the approach I prefer? Can I be patient as I allow others to enjoy the Lord's favor while I wait to do so myself? God's tastes are far wider than our own. What delights Him extends far beyond what we like.

Our release into the freedom of biblically authentic worship will allow the Lord to rejoice over us with singing and shouts of joy. Our understanding of the breadth of biblically authentic worship will allow the Lord to confide in us in a "still, small voice" and draw us to Him in the gentle quietness of contemplation.

The key to biblically authentic worship is to remember that it is all about Him...all for His glory...all for His delight...all to meet His design. Then when we see that He is pleased and honored, we will be delighted in the joy of the Father.

Show us the majestic splendor of the
holy God, and we will soon realize we
are wholly unlike Him.

The Lord your God is with you,

He is mighty to save. He will take

great delight in you, He will quiet

you with His love, He will rejoice

over you with singing.

Zephaniah 3:17 (NIV)

6

Delighting God's Heart in Worship

What, then, should take place in biblical worship? What needs to be involved when we come to praise the Lord? Certain key elements must be acknowledged as indispensable for true worship to take place, whether it is personal, family, or corporate worship. The whole of Scriptures teaches that there are several aspects of worship that must remain constant.

Biblical Worship Acknowledges Who God Is

Without the knowledge of who He is, our worship can become idolatrous as we slip into worship of false deities of our own imaginations rather than of the true God of biblical revelation. In every case, when the Bible describes an encounter between the living God and His people, the common denominator is always reverential awe and a healthy dose of the fear of the Lord. Time and time again, we find men and women who worship Him on their faces, bowed down low before Him. He is the Lord; He is holy. All true worship begins with a sense of holy awe as we enter the presence of the Almighty God Himself.

Biblical Worship Admits a Sense of Personal Unworthiness

Once we see Him as He is, it is a logical conclusion that we are totally unworthy of such an awesome God. Show us the majestic splendor of the holy God, and we will soon realize we are wholly unlike Him. Had He offered no further revelation than just allowing us to know that He is wholly beyond us and given us no hint of His redemptive intentions, we would be the most miserable of all creatures. Yet the Lord allows us to see Him and His glorious perfections so that we might recognize our neediness. Only as we comprehend how holiness and righteousness are found in Him alone can we admit we have no right to expect Him to receive anything we offer, our worship included. It is that sense of unworthiness and an awareness of our personal destitution that compel us to approach Him with all humility.

Biblical Worship Approaches God in Confidence

As members of His family, Christ has given us authority to confidently approach God's throne in His name (John 14:13-14; Hebrews 10:19-22). Because of the nature of our unworthiness, it is essential that we accept God's provision of a Mediator who will go before us and be our advocate. Knowing how far short of the mark we are makes it easy to understand the need for one who will intercede on our behalf. Such a One we have in Jesus Christ. He is the only Mediator worthy to stand between a holy God and a sinful human being. He alone died in our place, taking our unworthiness upon Himself in order to forgive us, cleanse us, and make us worthy in His own name. Therefore, our worship can only be acceptable when it is offered in the name of our Savior and Mediator, the Lord Jesus Christ.

Biblical Worship Requires Confession of Sin

Each time we come into the presence of the Lord, the slate must be clean. Therefore, although provision has been made for our forgiveness and cleansing, the provision must be appropriated. No honest observer of the human race should ever be surprised that sin frequently gains the upper hand in our lives. It happens often enough that we cannot afford to trivialize our offenses before the Lord and expect our worship relationship with Him not to suffer.

Therefore, an increasing awareness of the holiness of God through our growing knowledge of Him through Christ and His Word makes us ever more sensitive to the constant barrage of temptations and enticements to sin. One of the marks of maturity in growing believers is their sensitivity to the presence of sin in their lives. Confession of that sin must precede true worship so that its presence does not impede true worship.

Biblical Worship Expresses Praise and Thanksgiving

Words that express our gladness and appreciation to the Lord for who He is and what He has done should be part of every worship experience. Times for reflection and meditation prepare us for worship. As we take time to recall His grace in our lives, we are reminded of the distinctive aspects of His character, His attributes. Then we can sincerely praise Him for who He is and thank Him for what He has done.

Efforts at worship that fail to offer reminders and instruction about the character of the Lord, either in song or in various kinds of instruction, will prove to be shallow and without substance. Emotionalism and manipulative choreographed events may generate positive feelings within us about God, but we will never effectively worship the Lord until we praise Him for who He has revealed Himself to be and thank Him for all that He has done.

Biblical Worship Welcomes Instruction and Produces Grateful Obedience

Since Jesus said that we are to worship Him in spirit and truth, a portion of our worship must be set aside for instruction in the truths of the Lord and teaching from the Word of God. Without that instruction, our worship will not be informed, substantive worship. Following that instruction, there also should be time for personal commitments to be made as we present ourselves to Him, living sacrifices ready to live according to His revealed will. Never should we come away from worship the same way we came in. Entering into the presence of the Lord results in changed lives! Discovering more of Him as His truth is opened deeper through instruction empowered and illuminated by the Holy Spirit forms the proper basis for worship that progresses from words of praise to lives of grateful obedience.

Biblical Worship Is Filled with Psalms, Hymns, and Spiritual Songs

When we find people filled with the Spirit of the Lord, people who have allowed the Word of God to enrich their lives, the resulting joy and overwhelming impressions of awe find expression in musical ways, according to the Scriptures. Worship that is filled with a sense of God's presence will also be worship that makes a "joyful noise unto the Lord" (Psalm 66:1; 88:1 KJV) in songs of praise, songs of personal testimony, and songs of affirmed faith in a faithful Lord.

As Christ's lovely Bride, every church should want to become a people of true worship who love to come before the Lord and bow down humbly in His presence, offering themselves to Him as living sacrifices, which is every believer's spiritual service of worship (Romans 12:1-2). Those who are true worshipers long for Him and will let nothing diminish or trivialize their pursuit of His presence or proclamation of His praise! In a day when many in the body of Christ are busy arguing over which form is correct and which approach is more appropriate, Jesus appeals to all of us to come and worship...on His terms.

Americans have now embraced tolerance as their highest national value and compel everyone to accept every philosophy as equally valid. Is it right then, to continue to warn people that "the bridge is out just ahead," even when they demand to believe that it will not affect them? Of course it is!

For there is one God, and one mediator also between God and men, the man Christ Jesus.

1 Timothy 2:5

7

Defining Biblical Evangelism

During our seminary days, my wife Cathy and I lived about an hour from Salem, Massachusetts, a town notorious for the Witch Trials of the Puritan days in early American history. Although accounts of what happened largely depend upon the perspective of the writer, the accusations of a few young people in the colony provoked some rather radical responses among the community leaders. Soon wholesale accusations divided the community and resulted in what has come to be known as a "witch hunt."

The vocabulary of our nation expanded to include the phrase "witch hunt" as a way to describe any attempt to identify lifestyles and ideas that deviate from the norm. Books have been written, films and plays produced, and university courses taught condemning any effort made to point the finger at someone who dares to take a different course. Americans have now embraced tolerance as their highest national value and compel everyone to accept every philosophy as equally valid.

Sadly, many within the Church have also embraced this value and decried what they believe to be a narrow view of life. The prevailing sentiment seems to be "live and let live." Let people believe what they want. What gives Christians the right to push what they believe on others anyway? Is it right then, to continue to warn people that "the bridge is out just ahead," even when they demand to believe that it will not affect them?

Of course it is! Jesus Christ cried out for us to hold a much higher value – the glory and honor of His name. We must never be intimidated into silence as we seek to speak His name.

As we now turn to the biblical principles of evangelism, we are reminded that our overall purpose is to glorify God. In the previous chapters, we discussed how the content of our ministry must always include a steadfast commitment to worship the Lord in spirit and in truth. The second commitment we must make is to evangelism, reaching out to searching people who are apart from Christ so that they will know Him.

Unfortunately, the evangelism ministry of the body of Christ is usually the easiest to neglect and the quickest to be misunderstood. Unless it is regarded in its proper context, evangelism either dominates all other church ministries or is relegated to the other extreme – it is ignored. What must we do then in order to glorify God in evangelism? And how do we do it?

A study of the evangelistic practices of the earliest churches in the New Testament reveals the answers to three important questions:

- Where Is Our Evangelistic Field?
- What Is Our Evangelistic Message?
- What Is Our Evangelistic Strategy?

These principles not only set the course for the evangelistic ministry of the Church, but they also provide direction for individuals to effectively communicate the message of salvation through Jesus Christ.

Where Is Our Evangelistic Field?

Where should we focus our attention when we as the body of Christ reach out to those who do not know Him? Not all churches agree on the answer. Different emphases can be found in the wonderful diversity of the body of Christ, but all approaches must be traced back to the instructions Jesus gave to His disciples in Acts 1:8: "But you shall receive power when the Holy Spirit has come upon you; and you shall be My witnesses both in Jerusalem, and in all Judea and Samaria, and even to the remotest part of the earth."

Whatever the particular emphasis might be for a body of believers, it must address its evangelistic ministry to all three areas of need found in these words of Christ. Not all of them need to receive equal emphasis, but each must receive a proportional part of the outreach strategy of the Church. What are these areas for the Church today?

"In Jerusalem" – Our Own Community

As Jesus spoke, the disciples were in Jerusalem, and He instructed them to do the work of evangelism right where they were. This target area for evangelism means that each church has a responsibility to reach out to its own community, its own city, to proclaim the good news of Christ. Whether it is proclaimed to non-Christians who don't attend church, non-Christians who do, or to nominal Christians, it is the calling of every body of believers to evangelize its own "Jerusalem."

"In Judea and Samaria" – Our Own Culture

Jesus never intended for the gospel to remain a distinctively "Jerusalem experience." So He further directed His disciples to take the message out to the surrounding areas, to Judea and Samaria. These places were within the same general cultural setting but geographically removed from Jerusalem. In our situation, that commission extends our responsibility beyond our own city to the entire American culture.

"In the Remotest Part of the Earth" – Our World at Large

All parts of the world are included in Jesus' directive for where the Church must extend the ministry of evangelism. The Church cannot be complacent about any approach to evangelism that does not include a strategy to reach even the uttermost parts of the earth with the message of salvation.

The evangelistic field of the body of Christ includes all three areas, and the Church cannot relinquish its calling to be faithful in fulfilling the Great Commission throughout the world. Some churches, with a great vision for worldwide evangelism through missions, have missed the mandate to witness to the grace of Christ Jesus right in their own communities. Others have concentrated so intensively on their own communities that the broader needs of the world have suffered.

When we commit ourselves to follow Christ, we commit ourselves as His body to take our direction from the Head and to fulfill the entire Commission, with attention given to each field of evangelism.

The Church as an Evangelistic Base of Operation

Throughout the New Testament, we see that the evangelistic thrust of the body of Christ was based in the local church setting. Even as Paul and Barnabas began their itinerant evangelism trips as the earliest missionaries, they were commissioned and sent forth from a local church (Acts 13:1-4).

When churches through the centuries began to neglect their responsibility in this area, the Lord always arranged for the gospel to continue to go forth. In our day, we have seen that more and more institutions, which call themselves churches, have laid aside the mandate of evangelism. Hundreds of people with whom we have talked with in the course of ministry at Providence have expressed dismay, confusion, and sometimes indignation after hearing the gospel for the first time and then realizing that they have spent their lifetimes attending churches where they never heard the good news of salvation in Christ.

In the face of such a tragic failure, many parachurch groups have arisen to stand in the gap and proclaim what thousands of churches would not. God has blessed many of these ministries with great success because they have been faithful to His Word in what they have shared. Groups like Campus Crusade for Christ, Navigators, InterVarsity Christian Fellowship, Young Life, Youth for Christ, Fellowship of Christian Athletes, and dozens of others have been used mightily by the Lord to bring millions of people to Christ, both at home and overseas.

We are eternally grateful for their vision and commitment to the ministry of evangelism that was given by Christ to His people. Still, the fact remains that they are necessary only because churches have so miserably failed to carry on with their charge to preach Christ in all the earth. Therefore, in principle, we see that the Church is still the starting point for the evangelistic effort intended by Christ to reach communities and the world. The parachurch groups, then, function most consistently with their New Testament commission when they work alongside their brothers and sisters in the body of Christ, never in competition with them.

At Providence, we have been unusually blessed to have wonderful relationships with representatives of many parachurch ministries. One of the strengths of their ministry is found in their commitment to the local body as their base of operation, the equipping center, within which they can be loved and nurtured as they do the work to which Christ has called them.

In summary, the evangelistic field of the Church is always to be threefold – in Jerusalem, in Judea and Samaria, and to the remotest parts of the earth. Our responsibility then is to develop a ministry of evangelism, through the local body of believers, that zealously prepares and plans for ways to impact the community, both locally and worldwide, with the gospel of Jesus Christ. We cannot leave the job to the parachurch ministries, but must move to the front lines ourselves and be found faithful through the Church as the starting point for evangelism.

What Is Our Evangelistic Message?

What is so urgent about the message which Christ has entrusted to us that He would place such an emphasis on seeing it proclaimed worldwide? Simply put, it is because the gospel message has the power to change lives.

Yet so many churches downgrade the essential nature of the gospel and the uniqueness of salvation by grace through faith in Christ. Therefore, the need for declaring the gospel's distinctive message is greater than ever. We will never take seriously His command to go and tell others anywhere, much less everywhere, if we are not convinced that a person can only be saved from the condemnation of sin through the redemptive work of Christ's sacrificial and atoning death on the cross.

When we are convinced of the uniqueness of the gospel, we cannot help ourselves. We will make the message known out of compassion and compulsion. Our compassion moves us to tell others of Christ because we know how desperate and hopeless the sinner's condition is apart from God's forgiveness. Likewise, we are compelled to proclaim the message because we are moved by Christ's love for us and want to do what brings pleasure to His heart.

As we look deeper into the evangelistic message, we find three biblical principles that should shape the evangelistic ministry of the body of Christ.

The Content of the Message Must Always Be Christ

The power of the gospel is always seen when the message of the cross is preached. The apostle Paul summarized his ministry style best when he told the church in Corinth, "We preach Christ crucified, to Jews a stumbling block, and to Gentiles foolishness" (1 Corinthians 1:23). That essential message of the death of Christ for sinners never changes.

Regardless of the times, the cultural distinctives, or the geographical differences, the message of the gospel does not need to be adjusted to fit the circumstances. The common malady of the human condition is sin, no matter the setting. The message is always the same. Paul was so firm on this point that he pronounced those who changed or distorted the gospel accursed (Galatians 1:8-9.)

Accommodation has become such a primary value in our culture that it has replaced the integrity of maintaining the truth of the gospel. The history of missions is filled with stories of syncretistic and mutant religions, which have the properties and beliefs of several religions into which certain parts of the gospel were blended almost inconspicuously. With the noble ideal of being inoffensive to non-Christians, the perpetrators of a watered-down version of the gospel instead do terrible harm – offering millstones rather than living bread to people starving spiritually (Matthew 18:6).

Even worse is the offensive nature of such deviation from the gospel to the God of grace, who paid dearly with the life of His only begotten Son for the purity and efficacy of the message. The content of the message must always be preserved.

The Bearers of the Message Are His People

With all the wisdom of the ages, with the infinite omniscience that dwells only in the mind of God, He has established that the message of the gospel is to be proclaimed by His people. In other words, the message must have messengers to be heard:

> *"How then shall they call upon Him in whom they have not believed? And how shall they believe in Him whom they have not heard? And how shall they hear without a preacher? And how shall they preach unless they are sent? Just as it is written, 'How beautiful are the feet of those who bring glad tidings of good things!'" (Romans 10:14-15)*

The evangelistic church cannot accomplish its purposes by remaining content within the walls of its own building. A vision for evangelism must always look for ways to commission people from within to move out and to take the message of Christ beyond the limited sphere of influence we can have as the gathered body of Christ. We see the most effective work of evangelism being done in the New Testament after the church was scattered, sometimes through persecution, sometimes at the Spirit's prompting, but always spreading out and taking the message to people who had not heard of, or responded to, Christ.

As much as we would enjoy staying together to enjoy the sweet communion of the saints and the fellowship of the Spirit, we must maintain a "sending mentality." We gather in order to equip ourselves to be sent. Whether the sending mentality results in short-term projects (to establish a new work, encourage an existing work, or provide necessary human resources to do large tasks), permanent commissions (members becoming career missionaries or working in other vocational ministries), or simply provides the financial and prayer support base for those who can and do go, we have an awesome responsibility to send forth messengers constantly in order to continue functioning as an evangelistic church.

We, as the messengers, are simply the bearers of that which has been entrusted to our care. We are then responsible for delivering the message as we received it in accordance with God's Word. How amazing it is that God has placed such a treasure in the hearts and on the lips of His people!

The Range of the Message Must Be Impartial

As we go forth in Jesus' name to bear the message, we are called to take the message to everyone, everywhere. Partiality and discrimination have no place among those who are called to be citizens in the Kingdom of God, but this is especially true when it comes to the range of the message. There should never be a person or place to which a believer would not go to share the good news of life in Christ.

If we have enmity or prejudice against others, we must confess it in the presence of the Father so that no barrier to the proclamation of the gospel remains. If there are cultural, national, political, racial, or any other kinds of barriers that prevent us from going to someone to tell them about Christ, we are living in violation of the very message we proclaim.

The Lord Jesus Christ expects the Church to reach out and extend hope to everyone, everywhere, in His name. Encourage your church to have the same attitude as Paul when he wrote:

> "For I am not ashamed of the gospel, for it is the power of God for salvation to everyone who believes, to the Jew first and also to the Greek." (Romans 1:16)

With such a message, the body of Christ can march forth boldly and confidently, knowing that when we speak in His name, He unleashes "power from on high" and takes His truth straight to the hearts of those who need to hear and to believe in Him (Luke 24:49).

Strategically, we need to be more direct
in our plan to go where the "lost sheep" are
found, and not expect them to wander
into our pasture.

So he [Paul] was reasoning in the synagogue

with the Jews and the God-fearing Gentiles,

and in the marketplace every day with those

who happened to be present.

Acts 17:17

8

Developing an Evangelistic Strategy

Do you remember the first time someone tried to share Christ with you outside the context of a church service? For many of us, our memories of such encounters are not always pleasant. Visions of being put on the spot, embarrassed by the confrontation, still linger in my mind.

When I was still young, my church was quite evangelistic with strong gospel messages and appeals from the pulpit in every church service. Still with that background, I remember going downtown with my parents on a Saturday shopping trip and being shocked to see a man from our church standing on the street corner preaching. Few people were listening but he did not seem to be put off by that as he shouted his message so that he could be heard as much as a block away. I was afraid to get near him for fear he might ask me to join him!

As the years have gone by, I have been approached many times by people who wanted to tell me about Christ – sometimes in gracious ways but other times rudely and offensively. Similar experiences have turned many of us off to the idea of taking the initiative to communicate the gospel to others. We are so afraid of getting out on a limb in being an offensive witness that most of us never go near the tree!

Can we find a way to communicate without the rudeness or offensiveness that turned us off at one time or another? Now that we have discussed the evangelistic field and the evangelistic message, we turn our attention to developing an evangelistic strategy, our next biblical principle of evangelism. What does the Bible say about communicating the gospel clearly?

What Is Our Evangelistic Strategy?

In the ministry of the church, intentional plans and strategies are employed to bring about the desired result. Whether in budgeting, building, or recruiting leaders for various classes and ministries, certain strategic principles must be engaged or the outcome will be altered from the original intent. Yet, in evangelism, we seldom give much thought to strategy and the principles behind that strategy. Somehow we believe that people will just share their faith naturally with others, and we can direct our most creative thoughts and innovative work toward more critical areas of need. Experience proves that not to be the case. The following key principles are necessary in the field of evangelism if we hope to be effective in reaching people for Christ.

We Must Forge Out Into the World

It is not uncommon for Christians to view evangelism as a narrowly defined practice of the church. Some people believe that the responsibility of individual church members is to bring non-Christians to the church meetings, where they can hear an evangelistic sermon and then be invited to respond to Christ. Therefore, the person responsible for proclaiming the gospel is the preacher or the evangelistic speaker. Gospel proclamation is thought to be best left in the hands of the "professionals." At least that seems to be the logical conclusion of a significant percentage of church members.

The New Testament pictures evangelism quite differently. The body of Christ is to be found in the world, among the lost, leading them to know Christ in the context of their daily lives, not by cajoling them to come to church meetings so that they can be saved. Strategically, we need to be more direct in our plan to go where the "lost sheep" are found, and not expect them to wander into our pasture.

We Must Follow Through With Our Lives

The effectiveness of our corporate and individual witness depends upon the authenticity of the message in our own hearts and lives. Two parts accompany each testimony as it goes forth: the practical and the verbal. Living the Christian life with integrity and purity adds a practical dimension to our witness.

Too many times the message of words has already been undermined by the message of ungodly behavior. Non-Christians have every right to ask that we demonstrate the power of the gospel in our own lives before they make any commitment.

Unfortunately, the practical witness of living the Christian life frequently becomes an end in itself. For the testimony of Christ to be complete in our lives, it must not only have practical visibility, but it must be accompanied by verbal expression. We must not only live the life, but we must also explain to others how we received that life and then how they can receive eternal life in Jesus Christ. Our witness must be both practical and verbal if we hope to be effective instruments in personal and corporate evangelism.

We Must Be Focused on All Ages

When we decide to act, the primary target group for our evangelistic effort should be all ages, not solely adults or solely children. In the New Testament, the ones who were approached with the gospel were adults, and then entire households were reached. We have witnessed an inversion of that practice in recent decades, as children have become the primary target for evangelism. Jesus welcomed the little children and invited them to come to Him, a practice we should imitate with gladness, but some churches have chosen to focus almost exclusively on children in their evangelistic efforts.

There could be many reasons for this change in direction. Children are less threatening, less hardened in their worldview, and usually more accessible. Yet the issue at stake is whether or not churches are ready to redirect their outreach efforts toward all ages – choosing not to avoid those who may be harder to reach, but recognizing that everyone needs the Lord.

We Must Be Faithful to the Message

The strategy of the local body of believers should always be true to the message of the gospel and never compromise it in an attempt to be relevant or inoffensive. Watered-down versions of the gospel, which conveniently omit the harder portions, are also frequently stripped of saving efficacy. We cannot leave out the truth of man's sinfulness, the total inability of man to save himself, the necessity of an atoning sacrifice (the message of the cross), or any other truths that encompass the story of God's amazing grace.

We must be faithful messengers. We must work diligently to find ways to communicate that message in the most effective way possible. Words that would communicate to someone highly trained in technology or science would probably not be as meaningful to an everyday laborer. Likewise, ideas and illustrations of the message that would be meaningful to an adolescent would probably fail to strike a responsive chord in a senior citizen.

Everyone needs to be able to hear the message in words that communicate effectively, and without compromise, the truth of the gospel. The evangelistic strategy of the local body of believers must be based upon sound biblical principles and practical, creative methods that will serve the cause of Christ best, with efforts led and empowered by the Holy Spirit.

We have examined three categories of principles of evangelism: the evangelistic field, the evangelistic message, and the evangelistic strategy. With these three categories in mind, we can understand more fully why the evangelistic ministry of the Church must receive prayerful and wise planning in order to be used mightily by God to bring many to the saving knowledge of Christ. We can reasonably expect tremendous opposition from the enemy when we take seriously Christ's commission to evangelize, but this resistance should compel us to be prepared on our knees, in our hearts, in our minds, and then onward into action.

Much of our message has been invalidated by
our failure to live up to our claims that Christ
makes a difference in our lives.

I do not nullify the grace of God,

for if righteousness comes

through the Law,

then Christ died needlessly.

Galatians 2:21

9

Evangelism in Action

The nineteenth-century American evangelist, D. L. Moody [1] *was once approached* by one of his critics who said, "Mr. Moody, I do not appreciate or like the way you do evangelism." Moody responded by asking, "I am sorry to hear that. How do you do it?" The man sheepishly replied, "Well, I don't." Moody concluded the discussion by saying, "I like my way better!"

People are usually very quick to criticize the evangelistic methods of others but seldom propose an alternative approach that has proven to be effective in leading people to Christ. Although I was put off by the methods of the street preacher I encountered as a child, at least he was doing something while I was doing nothing!

Where would the witness of the body of Christ be if the majority voted by their actions and the general neglect of evangelism in the Church became the rule for all? Facing facts, we as evangelicals are much better at talking about evangelism than we are at doing anything about it. Yet no serious student of the Scriptures questions the high priority given to evangelism in the New Testament. The problems arise when evangelism does not have that same priority in the practical realm in our lives. We believe in it, we affirm the need for it, we are thankful someone shared Christ with us, but we are not always ready to take the steps necessary to be active participants in the ministry of evangelism.

When Christians speak of those without Christ, they often refer to them as "lost." With all the emphasis on politically correct language, the

---

1 D. L. Moody was an American evangelist who was the founder of Northfield Schools of Massachusetts, Moody Church, and the Moody Bible Institute in Chicago (born 1837-died 1899).

very word "lost" offends and suggests the possibility of a judgmental attitude on our part. As far as the terminology goes, the word still conveys exactly what it did to Jesus when He referred to the lost sheep without a shepherd, the lost coin sought until it was found, and the lost prodigal son who needed to find his way home. Lost people are people who have not found their way home to their Father's house and who wander aimlessly and hopelessly in search of that way.

In order to emphasize the need for evangelism and to encourage a deeper appreciation of the plight of those apart from Him, I find it helpful to define evangelism this way: Evangelism is reaching out to "searching people" with the truth about how to return to their Father's home. If we can begin to understand aberrant behavior and strange beliefs as products of searching hearts, we will be less intimidated and more inclined to answer their cry for someone to show them the Way.

Many words have been used to describe the condition of such people – desperate, wicked, aimless, violent, immoral, apathetic, belligerent – but as Christians we have far too often misinterpreted the noise of their misbehavior and missed the cry of their heart. Yet in most people, even those whom life has hardened and made cynical, a steady heartbeat of persistent searching continues:

- High school students who try on identities like blue jeans, trying to find the right fit.

- Men and women in mid-life crises who exchange the stability of job and home for the foolish trophies of worldly success.

- Fatherless boys who plead for someone to affirm and recognize their manhood, trying any way they can to assure themselves that their lives matter.

- Hopelessly poor people who try to claw their way out of their economic pit, unaware that if they succeed they will then suffer the futility of trying to fill another empty hole, this one hollowed out by the false promises of materialistic pleasure.

• Confused victims of cults as well as fanatical radicals of secular thinking vehemently defend the way they have chosen. Yet in moments of solitude, they cling to the hope that there must be something more than what they have.

These are searching people, not mean people, not our enemies, not menaces to the cause of Christ, but searching people who need someone to show them the way to Christ.

Christ commands us to be His witnesses. Our biblical and theological understanding of human depravity demands that we be His witnesses. Our identification of and familiarity with searching people all around us compel us to be His witnesses.

In the previous chapters, we examined biblical principles of evangelism, from the evangelistic field to the evangelistic message to the evangelistic strategy. Our focus now turns to the biblical principles of how to actually evangelize. What does an evangelistic church look like when it applies these biblical principles? The answer is found in two specific areas of evangelism:

As a Personal Witness – giving testimony to the message right where we are in our daily lives.

In Global Missions – sending forth the message beyond our immediate field of ministry.

As a Personal Witness

It was so important to God that we should be offered the opportunity to be forgiven, to find the Way of Life, and to know Him that He sent His own Son into the world. Christ came to purchase our pardon, to show us His way, and to proclaim a message of salvation: "For God so loved the world, that He gave His only begotten Son, that whoever believes in Him should not perish, but have eternal life" (John 3:16).

Every believer has been declared a witness for Christ in order that the dissemination of the gospel would carry on from generation to generation, never lacking an available voice. God's plan calls for us to tell searching people what we have found to be true, that salvation comes through faith in Jesus Christ. In general, that plan calls upon His people to proclaim a message, sometimes person-to-person and sometimes in public proclamation. To be effective witnesses, the Church needs to be equipped to do both.

A Personal Responsibility

For one person to share Christ with another, careful thought must be given to the subject if we hope to discover the most effective methods for each of us. We must understand more of what the Lord desires and overcome our own reticence to get involved. We also must understand that the effectiveness of our personal evangelistic approach will depend upon its practical validity. Six criteria must be met before determining whether the approach we take in personal evangelism actually works in our own lives.

1. **Comfort Level.** Would you be comfortable if someone used this approach with you?

2. **Effectiveness.** Are people actually coming to know Christ and walk with Him as a result of this approach to evangelism?

3. **Transferable.** Can this strategy be learned by others who can in turn reproduce the model in the lives of others?[2]

_____

2 "And the things which you have heard from me in the presence of many witnesses, these entrust to faithful men, who will be able to teach others also" (2 Timothy 2:2).

4. **Consistent.** Am I comfortable enough using this approach that I will continue to use it and incorporate it into my daily walk with Christ?

5. **Prayerful.** Does this strategy and approach seek the Lord and depend on Him in prayer or upon my own skills and abilities to convince people?

6. **Biblical.** Is what I am saying and doing consistent with and uncompromising with regard to the Scriptures?

Therefore, at Providence, we have adopted a strategy that addresses all of these concerns and has proven to be an effective means of involving significant numbers of believers in sharing Christ with others. We believe each member has a role to play in person-to-person witnessing that can be fulfilled by implementing a personal strategy that includes the following four basic commitments.

1. We must pray faithfully.

> *"Devote yourselves to prayer, keeping alert in it with an attitude of thanksgiving; praying at the same time for us as well, that God may open up to us a door for the word, so that we may speak forth the mystery of Christ, for which I have also been imprisoned; in order that I may make it clear in the way I ought to speak." (Colossians 4:2-4)*

Everyone knows people who are searching. If you believe those folks need someone to show them the way, you need to pray for them and for open doors so that they might hear and see the truth of the gospel. One of the ways we encourage our members to pray is to keep with them at all times a regular, updated prayer list of searching people who need to know Jesus Christ. As a matter of fact, with a small card in your wallet or purse, you can make it a matter of regular, faithful intercession to ask the Lord to show your friends or acquaintances the way to His Son. Who knows, He may allow you to lead them home!

2.   We must live authentically.

> *"Conduct yourselves with wisdom toward outsiders, making the most of the opportunity. Let your speech always be with grace, seasoned, as it were, with salt, so that you may know how you should respond to each person." (Colossians 4:5-6)*

If searching people want someone to show them rather than just tell them, we have to live more authentically, more genuinely, and with more integrity in the way we relate to others, inside and outside the Church. Much of our message has been invalidated by our failure to live up to our claims that Christ makes a difference in our lives. If there is no apparent difference because we are not living in a manner worthy of Christ, our credibility is lost. What we say must be backed up by what we do.

3.   We must care personally.

> *"But we proved to be gentle among you, as a nursing mother tenderly cares for her own children. Having thus a fond affection for you, we were well-pleased to impart to you not only the gospel of God but also our own lives, because you had become very dear to us." (1 Thessalonians 2:7-8)*

How much do you care personally for people who are still searching? Are you willing to get involved in their lives, giving up some of what is convenient and easy for you and showing others that you care? This means showing up where they are often enough so they notice that you keep coming back because you care. Searching people sense when they are your "project" and resent it or resist your intrusion into their world. But if you show them that you genuinely care and love them unconditionally, what matters to you will soon matter more to them. Your right to be heard is gained through a meaningful relationship – then you can show them the way for which they have been searching. Although you may meet initial resistance when you demonstrate love in action to someone, when combined with faithful prayer and genuineness in your life, the Lord will open a door for you.

4.   We must share clearly.

> *"Let your speech always be with grace, seasoned, as it were, with salt, so that you may know how you should respond to each person." (Colossians 4:6)*

Regardless of our other efforts, until we get around to explaining the gospel to searching people in words they can understand, they will never come to know Christ. With clarity and compassion, we must learn to share the gospel of Jesus Christ with those who need to know Him. We need to refine our communication skills and become familiar with the unique lifestyles, ideologies, and vocabularies of those with whom we speak. We must look for a way to connect with their hearts and minds.

Although the essence of the gospel message never changes, a wise witness never assumes that a "one-size-fits-all" approach works when trying to communicate to different people at various places along the way in their search. They need directions from where they are, not from where we wish they were. Our personal testimony is one effective tool that all believers have. Simply developing that unique resource provides an evangelistic approach that is personal, genuine, scriptural, and applicable. In the course of natural conversation, we must learn to speak clearly of Christ to those who are searching and need to understand that He alone is "the way, and the truth, and the life" (John 14:6).

As you can see, being effective in our witness for Christ and to searching people can become a normal expectation for every believer. Person to person, one by one, the body of Christ can show people the way to the Lord and allow the Spirit to conduct the work only He can do in bringing them to repentance, to faith in Christ, and to new life in His name!

In Public Proclamation

Beyond just the personal responsibility of personal witness, the Church must also engage in regular outreach efforts to proclaim the gospel in various public settings. Especially in the book of Acts, preaching the gospel was a central feature in the life of the early disciples. Whether in the synagogue, at the marketplace, by a river, in a jail cell, or before government authorities, every opportunity to declare the message of salvation through Jesus Christ was seized.

Many churches have yielded their times of corporate worship to evangelistic preaching, focusing not so much on leading believers into the presence of the Lord but rather on inviting unbelievers to come to salvation. Churches that have adopted this style of ministry have been criticized, sometimes unfairly, for becoming so "seeker sensitive" that they have forsaken genuine worship.

The priority given to public proclamation of the gospel in these churches cannot be faulted on biblical grounds since we see the early church adopting this practice with great success. However, the matter under scrutiny is whether evangelistic services of gospel preaching have replaced services of worship and adoration. I believe proponents of both perspectives have much to gain and little to lose by listening to each other.

Worship-focused churches, and even Bible-teaching churches, can more effectively proclaim the message of the gospel and invite searching people to respond to the offer of grace presented to them through Jesus Christ. Evangelistic churches would also do well to recognize the importance of worship as one of the most effective tools for reaching people for Christ.[3] When Christ is lifted up in praise and worship and when the presence of the Lord is joyfully celebrated by His people, great power is found in the promise of Jesus that when He is lifted up, He will "draw all men" unto Him (John 12:32).

---

3 See Sally Morgenthaler's *Worship Evangelism* (Grand Rapids, Michigan: Zondervan Publishing Company, 1995) for an extensive discussion of this point. Her emphasis is obvious from the subtitle, "Inviting Unbelievers into the Presence of God."

Churches that desire to fulfill not only the command to be personal witnesses, but to follow the pattern of public proclamation, can explore new and creative avenues for preaching and making known the gospel in a variety of settings. It is the challenge of our day, as it is in any era, to discover where and how – not whether – to publicly and faithfully announce the good news of salvation. Only our lack of boldness and our lack of imagination hold us back.

In Global Missions

Perhaps for many in the body of Christ, it is easier to accept the responsibility of the Church to engage in missions rather than in witness because at first appearance not as much personal commitment is expected. However, when the body of Christ is functioning as it should, each of us shares just as much responsibility for missions as we do for witnessing. At any given time in the life of the church, every member is expected to participate in missions to the extent that God enables them. Here are four specific ways the body of believers can become involved in missions.

1. We must pray.

> "*Devote yourselves to prayer, keeping alert in it with an attitude of thanksgiving; praying at the same time for us as well, that God may open up to us a door for the word, so that we may speak forth the mystery of Christ, for which I have also been imprisoned; in order that I may make it clear in the way I ought to speak.*" (*Colossians 4:2-4*)

Just as our responsibility as personal witnesses begins with praying faithfully, so does our responsibility for missions. Every church member must devote time to prayer for missions and missionaries. At Providence, we developed a missions team to help church members begin to pray for missions by providing them with excellent resources, contacts, awareness, etc. Ignorance should not be an excuse for your congregation. Be ready to provide information for your flock about ways to pray for missions and missionaries.

2. We must pay.

> *"For I testify that **according to their ability**, and **beyond their ability** they gave of their own accord, begging us with much entreaty for the favor of participation in the support of the saints, and this, not as we had expected, but they first gave themselves to the Lord and to us by the will of God."* (2 Corinthians 8:3-5)

Both the Church as a whole and the individual members have the responsibility to provide financially for missions from the regular tithes and offerings given weekly. The Church must lead the way in appropriating the funds necessary to give financial support for missions from the gifts of its members. Individuals should also consider giving over and above their regular tithes and offerings through the local congregation by increasing their giving to a sacrificial level in support of other missionaries than those for whom their church provides.

Many missionaries and missions depend upon individuals in addition to churches for their support. Without the generosity of individual believers to sustain their missionary efforts, most of them would be unable to remain in the field to which God has called them. Missions is a team effort that involves those who are called to go and those who are called to provide financial support.

In 2004, approximately 16 million Americans identified themselves as evangelical Christians.[4] If as few as one percent of them responded to God's call to missions and had the necessary funds to go where He called them to go, churches and individual believers would be supporting approximately 160,000 missionaries.

---

4 According to The Barna Group website, *www.barna.org,* "Research Archive, Evangelical Christians" accessed on 8/30/2004.

As it is, the 66,000 missionaries currently based in the United States,[5] who have already followed God's calling to missions, struggle to survive financially because of the limited availability of funds from their fellow believers in the churches.

Therefore, members should be supporting missions from their personal resources and churches from their corporate resources, in proportion to the pattern outlined in the Bible: "according to and beyond their ability" (2 Corinthians 8:3).

3. We must prepare.

> "All Scripture is inspired by God and profitable for teaching, for reproof, for correction, for **training** in righteousness; that the man of God may be adequate, **equipped** for every good work." (2 Timothy 3:16-17)

When God calls His people to go, He first calls them to prepare to go, a process that requires *training* and *equipping* so that their efforts will demonstrate the kind of excellence the Lord deserves. The word for "equipping" (exartizo) and the word "seasoned" (artuo) in Colossians 4:6 have the same root in the Greek, suggesting that we must be properly seasoned, prepared, and equipped to offer the most flavorful and effective witness for Christ.

Many have been called, but they became too impatient to prepare before they went out. Consequently, their lack of training and their inadequacies for the tasks required caused them to fail unnecessarily and give up prematurely. Had someone taken the time to train them, to hold them accountable to be equipped properly, the results could have been very different.

The Church needs to provide the kind of environment that nurtures and equips men and women for ministry. There is no substitute for

---

5 Patrick Johnstone, *Operation World* (Pasadena, California: United States Center for World Mission, 2001): 658.

preparing people for genuine Christian living by leading them toward maturity in Christ and training them in the skills of ministry.

When the body of Christ is doing its job right, there should be a steady pipeline of people who are ready to go at a moment's notice anywhere the Lord says. There is no need to send out those unsuited or untrained for service as long as the work of the ministry continues to produce committed men and women who long to be equipped to be laborers in the fields of the Lord.

4.   We must proceed.

> *"Then I heard the voice of the Lord, saying, 'Whom shall I send, and who will go for Us?' Then I said, 'Here am I. Send me!'" (Isaiah 6:8)*

Certainly the Lord has called many more than have responded to His call to missions. As the Lord clears the way and calls you forth, do not postpone your going until a more opportune time because that time may never come. The Lord wants to call people who are ready to get up and go, proceeding with the first steps of obedience as soon as His calling has been confirmed.

Like Isaiah, we need to be ready to respond immediately and with certainty, "Lord, here I am. Send me!" If the Lord calls you, by all means, get on with it! Proceed! Go! Then, as you go, remember the words of Christ: "Make disciples of all the nations, baptizing them in the name of the Father and the Son and the Holy Spirit, teaching them to observe all that I commanded you; and lo, I am with you always, even to the end of the age" (Matthew 28:19-20).

That is our Great Commission, given to each of us as His disciples, whether our witness is beyond the immediate geographical area or to our friends and neighbors in our hometown. What a privilege to be given the ministry of evangelism and to watch as the Lord uses people like us to show searching people the way home to Him!

When we become believers, the boundaries of
our family relationships immediately explode!

For you are all sons of God

through faith in Christ Jesus.

Galatians 3:26

Creating an Edifying Environment

Can you think of anything more persistent than a child with a question on his mind? If you have ever spent any time around young children, you know what happens when they don't understand something or happen to be curious about something. Or even more urgently, when they want you to give them something or to do something for them this instant!

As exasperating as it can be, we should try not to cut off the imaginative and innocent questions of a child. Sometimes they can go on and on, but it is vital that we encourage them to ask about what they do not know and to feel at home with us. Every good parent wants to create a loving environment for their children – a place where they can be safe, feel loved, and be encouraged to grow to maturity.

How much more then, does our heavenly Father, (who knows how to give good gifts to His children) desire to provide a place for us to be properly nurtured and to grow to maturity in Christ? (Matthew 7:11) John expressed it well when he said, "I have no greater joy than this, to hear of my children walking in the truth" (3 John 4).

As the ministries of worship and evangelism begin to bear fruit, the ministry of edification must be ready to preserve that fruit and to invest the gifts and resources of Christ's body in the wonderful process of building up its members to maturity. The Church's effectiveness can largely be measured by the degree to which its people are encouraged and enabled to walk in the truth, built up in their faith in Jesus Christ. But how does the Church as the body of Christ create an environment that will nurture and edify believers? A careful study of the New Testament reveals five facets of the environment God wants to create for edification. He wants the body of

Christ to be a covenant people, a functioning organization, a family place, an equipping center, and a maturing base.

The Body Is a Covenant People

As any parent knows, a stable secure environment is a critical element of nurturing children to healthy growth. It is important for children to know they are loved and that their parents will always love them and are committed to them no matter what. In the same way, our heavenly Father is a covenant-making God. He has entered into a covenant agreement with His people established by blood, the blood of His only Son. Jesus told His disciples that the cup He poured out for them on the night of His betrayal was the new covenant in His blood (Luke 22:20).

Unlike the old covenant, the new covenant would be written not on stones, but upon the hearts of His people: "I will put My laws into their minds, and I will write them upon their hearts. And I will be their God, and they shall be My people" (Hebrews 8:10). We are a covenant people because we have been brought into His family, we who are members of the body of Christ, by means of an eternal covenant initiated by the infinite love of our heavenly Father. He is eternally committed to us.

But how can young believers understand and be assured of that commitment? How can the eternal loving commitment of a covenant-keeping God be communicated to them? In order for His covenant people to work together for His glory and to maintain a stable edifying environment for believers, God ordained that three constants must remain in effect regardless of a congregation's size: servant-leaders, a large group structure, and a small group structure.

The Body of Christ Needs Servant-Leaders

The concept of leadership in the body of Christ that is exemplified by the New Testament church presents some real difficulties for our culture in the 21st century. Few models exist in a secular setting to aid in explaining the intent of biblical leadership. Why? Because leaders in the body of Christ must be servants.

How alien this concept is to the current practices of many churches! It becomes apparent all too quickly that the political processes at work in many churches are taken without amendment from the self-serving secular world with all of its maneuvering and manipulation preserved intact. Leadership roles have been redefined in our culture to reflect hierarchical patterns of autocracy rather than the biblical pattern of sacrificial service.

Spiritual leadership should always be servant leadership, based upon two foundations – character and trust. The character of the leader must match that of the Head of the body, so that the measure of one's suitability to lead within the Church is directly related to one's conformity to the character of Christ. Trust is then placed in such a leader by the people within the body who consent to pray for, and to follow, the servant-leader.

Spiritual leaders must function with the same attitude evident in Christ when He washed the dusty feet of His disciples in John 13. Our Savior established the priority of selfless leadership and told His disciples that the "Son of Man did not come to be served, but to serve, and to give His life a ransom for many" (Matthew 20:28).

Although there are innumerable ways for servant-leaders to serve the body of Christ, the Bible sets forth two distinct offices to be recognized and filled: the offices of deacons and elders.[1] Granted, leadership roles can never be restricted to just these two, nor should they be if spiritual gifts are properly exercised within the Church. However, these two positions are reserved for those who meet the biblical qualifications stated specifically in 1 Timothy 3 and Titus 1. Those selected must have demonstrated through their lives and ministries that they have matured in Christ to the point that they are seen by their peers as humble servants who would be faithful in leading the Church to follow Christ.

Servant-leaders are part of God's design for the effective ministry of a covenant people called by His name. These undershepherds lead the flock

---

1 For further discussion of the differences between the offices of elder and deacon, please see the appendix entitled "Most Frequently Asked Questions About Elder/Deacon Structure."

forward as they focus their eyes on and walk faithfully with the Shepherd Himself, Jesus Christ. Although it is abundantly clear from the Scriptures that no mediator but Christ is necessary for any believer to come to the Father, it is also clear that God's plan for His body includes servant-leaders who are held accountable for those allotted to their care (Hebrews 13:17).

The Body of Christ Needs Peoplehood (Large Groups)

When the early church arose in the days following Pentecost, the believers did not cease in their public worship practices. They continued to gather in the synagogues to worship the Lord, but they also began to meet on the first day of the week, the day of the resurrection. New believers were being added daily, and many of the Jewish leaders were coming to faith in Christ. Throughout Jerusalem, believers sensed they belonged to a mighty movement of God. The concept of peoplehood emerged and was fed through their regular gatherings in large groups to worship.

Two key words emphasize the importance of large group gatherings for the people of God: *celebration* and *identification.* As those who have been to large sporting events, concerts, or rallies can attest, a festive sense of celebration often permeates the atmosphere. So it is with a large group gathering of God's people. Gathering together fosters a joyful atmosphere as we assemble to celebrate His praise, marvel at His grace, and declare together that the Lord alone is God Most High. We also gain a sense of identity, a sense of belonging to a larger family, with a multitude of other believers we can relate to as brothers and sisters in Christ. Large group gatherings are a part of God's design for the Church as a covenant people.

The Body of Christ Needs Community (Small Groups)

From the earliest days of the church, the Lord also provided the need for small groups of believers to gather in His name. Right away in Jerusalem, the believers gathered together from house to house to devote themselves to the "apostles' teaching and to fellowship, to the breaking of bread and to prayer" (Acts 2:42). They understood what many in the Church today have either forgotten or never grasped: *Christians need each other.*

In these more intimate settings, the believers in Jerusalem could enjoy a level of growth that would otherwise have been lacking. Smaller groups enabled them to experience genuine community as a body of believers. Depth of sharing in one another's lives was possible because they were able to know each other on a more personal level. Accountability was also heightened. People who under other circumstances could get away with indiscreet behavior and inconsistent beliefs and practices were called to task by those close enough to know the truth about them. Community was critical to the edification of these believers, and so the Lord established a pattern of small groups in the early church as a model to follow in the centuries to come.

Therefore, these three elements must be present in order for the body of Christ to function properly as a covenant people:

- Servant-leaders who love Christ and His people more than leading

- Large groups to maintain our identity as a people and to celebrate our heritage in Christ

- Small groups to build community within the body and to foster a climate for growth impossible in any other setting

The Body Is a Functioning Organization

After responding to the call of Christ and entering into a covenant relationship with God, we soon realize the complexity of the body of which we are now a part. The human body is composed of intricate systems of interrelated parts and functions only when each part fulfills its purpose.

Similarly, the body of Christ must operate with individual parts functioning in an organized fashion with others in order to accomplish the purposes of Christ.

But extremes tend to develop whenever the finite mind of man takes what the infinitely wise mind of God has created and tries to "improve" upon His plan. Foolishly neglecting the wonderful balance of His design, we tend to drift into eccentric streams that lead us to develop strange practices alien to His intent. Therefore, balance and organization are essential to the Master's plan for His Church to function properly and to provide a solid, edifying environment for His people.

Is the Church an Organism or an Organization?

When the body neglects God's balanced design and errs on the side of freedom, it can rapidly slide from liberty into a libertine frame of mind. Out of the house church movement of the past thirty years in the United States, the philosophy adopted most frequently has been that the body of Christ is just a living organism. Those who hold this philosophy believe that as an organism, its life is to be unrestricted by the confinement of structures or organizational straitjackets. From this perspective, the life of Christ flowing through the people is all that matters. Any attempt to bring structure into such a free setting would do irreparable damage.

The first problem is that this ministry approach ignores the fundamental biblical principle of what constitutes the body of Christ, functioning under one Head. With no skeletal system, the human body would collapse on itself and be incapable of sustaining life. With no interdependence of the bodily systems that regulate and organize the vital organs, life would be impossible. For a living being to continue to live, it must have certain basic structures or it is no longer an organism. This is equally true for the Church.

Secondly, the body of Christ under the direction of its Head is expected to be obedient to His commands. With no structure, it is effectively paralyzed. Many of the house churches have ended up as self-serving entities with no real interest in reaching others for Christ or serving others in His name because, in order to do so, there must be some organization. In addition, the ministries given to the body of Christ require that certain spiritual gifts be exercised at various levels of leadership. Without leadership, these gifts would not be recognized and could not function as God intended. Granted, the concept of organism is critical to the life of the body, but God's design makes it impossible for it to function, or even to exist for long, without the balancing influence of organization.

The opposite extreme of this philosophy sees the Church as purely an organization. We see this extreme far more often as man's legalistic impulses draw the Church into a web of ever-expanding structures, policies, programs, committees, and procedures that eventually choke out all remaining vestiges of life in the organism. The net result is that the structure can remain long after the life has departed. Unfortunately, too many churches are so well organized that the presence or absence of the Holy Spirit makes little, if any, difference in what they do.

From these two extremes of organizational eccentricity, the institutional church has emerged as an easy target for anyone inclined to have an antichurch bias. The "all-structure-no-life" model perverts the testimony of the body as the place to experience abundant life in Christ by "holding to a form a godliness, although they have denied its power" (2 Timothy 3:5).

A healthy church must maintain a careful balance between the two extremes of organism and organization, enabling the body of Christ to function the way Christ intends. Later in Chapter 14, we will explore this facet in more detail as we discuss the flexibility and functionality that should be present in the structure of the Church.

The Body Is a Family Place

When we read in God's Word that the Lord wants to bring us into His family as children especially chosen by Him, the significance of His desire takes a while to sink in (John 1:12; Ephesians 1:3-5). Whether one's family experiences have been positive or negative, the idea that there is a place for each of us in an eternal family, where we can truly belong, is overwhelming. The implications of having a Father who loves and cares for us perfectly stagger our imaginations but motivate us to want to know more.

As those who have been adopted by God, we have the privilege of calling Him by the intimate name "Abba." We also know that, in the name of His Son, we have been granted a certain standing as children of God, which gives us acceptance in His presence. We are part of the same family with Jesus Christ and are therefore joint heirs, not only with Him, but with each other.

We belong to a family, a family comprised of those who are adopted by Christ, led by the Spirit, and baptized into the body of Christ. The Holy Spirit bears witness with our spirit that we are children of God "and if children, heirs also, heirs of God and fellow heirs with Christ" (Romans 8:17).

We Have an Extended Christian Family

I remember baptizing the first of my sons. As I prepared to lower him into the water, I looked into his eyes and said, "You are both my son and my brother!" When we become believers, the boundaries of our family relationships immediately explode! And regardless of where a believer goes in this world, family is always near.

Through frequent missions trips, I have had opportunity to meet brothers and sisters in the extended Christian family with whom I felt an instant kindred spirit. The extension of our family life to include such a wonderful array of the human race should excite every believer. Cultural, linguistic, geographic, and socioeconomic barriers fall before the Lord, who binds our hearts and knits us together into a family through His eternal love, a love demonstrated ultimately in Jesus Christ.

The joys of family life in the Church include the corporate experiences of praying, singing, sharing, serving, caring, giving, and even eating together, which are all important. Let us not forget that our earliest life experiences are molded by our home life. We walk, talk, and relate to others according to the models we have as infants, coming to grips with the vitality of life in this world. Therefore, we should expect our extended Christian family to provide the environment and model needed to have vital learning, relational, and witnessing experiences in the family of God. The Church needs to take seriously its role in providing the kind of healthy spiritual family life its members need to grow to maturity in Christ.

We Have a Healthy Nuclear Family

A significant part of the edification process of the local church is to encourage the development of a strong, Christ-centered, warm family life for every family represented in the body. Because so much of our lives is impacted by what happens within the framework of the nuclear family, the Church must be committed to providing the kind of support and instruction needed to help its people function biblically as families.

As families are disintegrating in every other level of our culture, the Church should be able to stand up and declare that in Christ Jesus, family life can be different! Unfortunately, the Church has conceded too much ground here. We must recapture what the enemy has stolen and equip the nuclear families within the family of God with the weapons of spiritual warfare to defend themselves. Encouraging the development of Christ-centered families will leave a godly heritage for generations to come.

Whenever the body of Christ teaches the
Word without teaching obedient action,
it does not equip the saints at all.

Equipping...the saints

for the work of service, to the

building up of the body of Christ.

Ephesians 4:12

11

The Church as an Equipping Center

Have you ever attempted some project that frustrated you completely because you did not have the right tools or equipment? When Hurricane Floyd swept through North Carolina in 1999, I found myself wishing I had some things I did not have. As I struggled to reach a broken second-story window, I wished I had a "real" ladder tall enough to do the job! Before the storm hit, I also wished I had one of those circular saw blades on the end of a long extension so that I could cut down some dangerous looking branches. As it turned out, I did my best with what I had but wished I had just the right tools and equipment to do what needed to be done.

Many folks live their lives feeling ill-equipped to face the various struggles that come their way. Each day seems to bring up some new issue that reinforces our basic inadequacy to handle what life throws at us.

However, that is not true for the follower of Jesus Christ. He has given us everything we need to live life to the fullest measure. God has given us His Word to equip us for all that life requires of us. The challenge for the Church is to provide a place to properly equip His children to face the challenges they will confront as believers in Christ.

In the previous chapters, we have already seen that the body of Christ is to be a covenant people, a functioning organization, and a family place. Now let's turn our attention to a fourth aspect God desires for His body.

The Body Is an Equipping Center

For many years, the Church fell into a pattern of ministry that viewed itself as an institution that met within a specific building once or twice a week to "do the Lord's work." Essentially, the "church gathered" was the church, and there was no practical concept of the "church scattered." When the meetings at the church site ended, for all practical purposes the church ceased to exist until the next scheduled meeting time at the building. Even now, when most people talk about "the church," they are referring to the building where the Church, the people of God, meets.

What a refreshingly different picture we find in the New Testament! In the Scriptures, "the Church" always refers to the body of Christ, His people. As we have reflected on the ministry of edification, we have had in mind those individual members who share life together under the authority of Christ. Therefore, when the Church gathers together, one of its functions is to serve as an equipping center for the members. Individuals come together as a corporate body to worship and to share in the fellowship of the Spirit, but they also come to be equipped to return to the world to live and serve in Jesus' name.

The following two passages have helped me understand this concept more than any others:

> *"And He gave some as apostles, and some as prophets, and some as evangelists, and some as pastors and teachers, for the equipping of the saints for the work of service, to the building up of the body of Christ." (Ephesians 4:11-12)*

> *"So that the man of God may be adequate, equipped for every good work." (2 Timothy 3:17)*

In the Ephesians passage, Paul names the special leaders given by God to the body of Christ and then explains that they have been given "for the equipping of the saints for the work of service." They are not charged with the responsibility of *doing* the work of service, but of *equipping* the saints for that purpose. How are they to equip the Church? With what tools will the saints be sent forth to do what God calls them to do? They are to be equipped with the Word of God. Since all Scripture is inspired by God, it is both effective in accomplishing that for which it is sent and trustworthy in what it says. Paul later tells Timothy that the Word is given so "that the man of God may be adequate, equipped for every good work" (3:17).

In these two passages, the Bible clearly states that the people of God, the saints, are to be equipped. God fully intends that all believers be made adequate, sufficient, for those things that they are called to do. The Church, then, is seen as an equipping center, where leaders in the body equip the members for their ministries by teaching them God's Word. What a wonderfully simple plan, but how neglected in so many churches!

In order for this part of His plan to be implemented, three issues must be addressed for believers to be equipped.

Believers Need Basic Knowledge of the Faith

Every member of the body of Christ must be given instruction in the fundamentals of faith in Christ. No one should be permitted to languish in ignorance regarding the great assurances secured for each believer by the Lord Jesus. When welcoming members into the household of faith, one of the Church's priorities is to introduce them to the biblical basics about what it means to belong to Christ.

For example, they need to know about the excellencies of Jesus Christ, the nature and depth of man's natural sinful condition, the wonderful freedom of the atonement and forgiveness, the trustworthiness and authority of the Scriptures, the abiding presence of Christ and the indwelling of the Holy Spirit, the privilege of prayer, and many other such basic issues woven through the pages of God's Word.

Believers Need Basic Bible Study Principles

Next, new believers must be shown how to go beyond the basics of their new birth into the daily joys of living and growing to maturity in Christ. In the earliest stages of growth, new believers thrive on "spoon-feeding," so they love to hear exciting preachers and teachers. However, the Church would do a great disservice to these new believers if they were kept dependent upon others for food forever. The responsibility of every parent is to train children to grow up and learn to feed and nurture themselves. The body of Christ must be an equipping center that arms believers with basic Bible study principles, so they can learn the joy of discovering gems of God's truth for themselves.

As the Church grows, it must continue to teach the truths of God's Word in such a way that the members develop a hunger for the meat, not just the milk, of the Bible. Milk will sustain certain levels of life, but the more actively the people pursue their walk with Christ, the more they will need the nourishment of more mature food.

Eventually, the Church must develop and teach Bible study principles to the members so that they can learn for themselves how to gain in-depth knowledge of God's Word through their own personal study. They will then know what it is to feed on the eternal truths of the Lord, and they will be ready to teach others, as they have been taught. Only then will the body of Christ continue to be equipped for ministry.

Believers Need Practical Application

Success in most endeavors requires both teaching and training. If you are going to succeed in playing a musical instrument, you must invest time in the classroom learning the basic structures of music. However, if your teacher only instructs you in music theory but never in how to actually hold and play the instrument, you will never succeed, no matter how well you understand the theory!

Every new biblical truth, taught or discovered, should be met with the question, "So what?" The Church must provide believers with opportunities and challenges to apply what they are learning in the daily affairs of their lives. Biblical truths and principles without any roots in practical daily living become nothing more than a basis for puffed-up minds and haughty spirits. God's Word is always intended to compel His people to act. Whenever the body of Christ teaches the Word without teaching obedient action, it does not equip the saints at all.

In summary, equipping the saints for service means giving them a basic knowledge of the faith, study principles for growth, and practical applications that encourage obedience. Believers who have been thus equipped will soon find their lives transformed by the power of biblical truth. Well-prepared and armed with their confidence in God and His faithfulness, they will eagerly go forth as laborers to His harvest.

The Body Is a Maturing Base

When you were a teenager, did your parents ever say to you (usually in exasperation), "It's time to grow up"? Just like any parent, our heavenly Father wants us to grow up – that is His goal. The apostle Paul understood this truth as he wrote:

> "But speaking the truth in love, **we are to grow up** in all aspects into Him, who is the Head, even Christ, from whom the whole body, being fitted and held together by that which every joint supplies, according to the proper working of each individual part, causes the growth of the body for the building up of itself in love." (Ephesians 4:15-16)

The whole idea of edification declares that the people of God who are born into His family need to grow up, need to be built up, and need to mature. The body of Christ provides the base for that to happen. The maturity and growth within the body that delights the heart of Christ reflects His character in the lives of His people.

This kind of growth builds upon a foundation the Scriptures call the Cornerstone and draws its vitality from the dynamic life of the living stone:

> "And coming to Him as to a living stone, rejected by men, but choice and precious in the sight of God, you also, as living stones, are being built up as a spiritual house for a holy priesthood, to offer up spiritual sacrifices acceptable to God through Jesus Christ.

For this is contained in Scripture: BEHOLD, I LAY IN ZION A CHOICE STONE, A PRECIOUS CORNERSTONE, AND HE WHO BELIEVES IN HIM WILL NOT BE DISAPPOINTED." (1 Peter 2:4-6)

The two greatest evidences of maturity are the desire within our hearts to worship Him and the depth of our commitment to serve Him and others. Mature worship and mature service are the marks of churches that have embraced their walk with Christ with sincerity and seriousness. These believers wholeheartedly long to grow in all the fullness of the Lord.

Maturity will always move in an outward direction after the inner workings of the Holy Spirit reproduce something of the character of Christ in our hearts. Therefore, serving others should naturally follow as the believer begins to have a heart for others, which was evident in the earthly ministry of Jesus Christ.

If we follow the Master, we will also find ourselves humbled, bowed down as we do things for the sake of others:

"Truly, truly, I say to you, a slave is not greater than his master; neither is one who is sent greater than the one who sent him. If you know these things, you are blessed if you do them." (John 13:16-17)

Mature servants give no thought to their own recognition and do not call attention to their service, nor do they serve only when it is convenient for them to do so. They serve with humble hearts and understand the reality of their position before the Lord. Selfishness and preoccupation with self-interest have no place in the hearts of those who are being made complete, who are growing up in all aspects into Christ, the living Head of the body. In a culture that runs on the fuel of self-interest, the very idea of living for a purpose beyond ourselves sounds noble but proves to demand a higher price than many are willing to pay. Yet Christ's desire is that all who see His Church will declare, "Behold how they love one another" (John 13:34-35).

Christ longs for His Church to be a nurturing environment, a place where His children can be edified and grow to maturity. He wants us to recognize that we are His covenant people, a functioning organization, a family place, an equipping center, and a maturing base – so that each believer will enjoy the wonders of growing up to maturity in Christ.

So far, however, we have only discussed the "theory" of edification. The topic of our next chapter is learning how to actually practice it!

Healthy growth requires that we recognize
our need for each other and accept our
individual responsibility to work toward
mutual maturity in Christ.

That I may be encouraged

together with you while among you,

each of us by the other's faith,

both yours and mine.

Romans 1:12

12

Keys for Edification

A few years ago, I used to drive by a construction site where a large building had been started but stalled. For months after the first couple of block walls had gone up, nothing else was done. Like many others who passed that way, I could not help but wonder what had happened. Had they run out of money, or had the contractor quit, or were there new owners who had changed their minds about building? A project underway with no visible progress seems to leave an unsettled feeling in all who pass by.

Sometimes I am sure that the Lord would love to put a sign around our necks that says, "Be Patient. Work in Progress." What He has begun in the lives of those who belong to Him He has committed to complete, but along the way some of us have a tendency to stall the progress!

As His Church, He is committed to growing us to maturity. Yet many have no interest in growth, no desire to mature, and are quite willing to let the construction site sit as an unfinished mess. God calls us to continue to be built up in Him until we are mature in Christ. He wants us to grow up. He wants us to be different tomorrow than we are today. He wants to see more of His character in His Bride and less of ours. In order to grow to maturity in Christ, God calls on us to build one another up, to edify one another.

If a church is not committed to edification, it will never accurately reflect the Lord because it will not progress toward the kind of complete and mature character He expects. Paul explains that we are to grow up in all aspects of Him who is the Head of the body. Furthermore, he says we need each other in this process. As we allow the Holy Spirit to work within us, the whole body of Christ "grows and builds itself up in love, as each part does its work" (Ephesians 4:15-16 NIV).

Healthy growth requires that we recognize our need for each other and accept our individual responsibility to work toward mutual maturity in Christ. Edification encompasses many aspects of the growth process.

PRAYER
RELATIONSHIPS
INSTRUCTION
SERVICE
MANAGEMENT

All members must be committed to God's plan for their edification by faithfully engaging in each of these areas. When we neglect our part, the whole body suffers. Membership, then, carries great responsibility since the body of Christ will be built up only "according to the proper working of each individual part" (Ephesians 4:16).

The Ministry of Prayer

If ever there was a case to be made for the benefits of a monologue rather than a dialogue, God has one! When He speaks, we should listen and obey. Yet He has not created us to be only recipients of divine edicts. God wants communication with His people and has established a way for that conversation to be a two-way street. He speaks to us in His Word and then invites us to respond in prayer. This holy dialogue constitutes one of the highest privileges ever extended to the human race.

How can we edify one another in the ministry of prayer? The Scriptures give us a few clues. The ministry of prayer in the body of Christ should include the following:

- Praying together continually and fasting, as the need arises, in special seasons of prayer (Acts 2:42, 4:31)

- Teaching one another how to pray and regularly exhorting each other to pray (Luke 11:1-4)

- Interceding for others in small group and large group times of prayer; confessing our personal, congregational, and national sins; and exalting the name of the Lord with praise and thanksgiving (Nehemiah 9:2-3; 1 Chronicles 29:10-20)

- Organizing efforts of continual intercession to develop a corporate practice of praying without ceasing (1 Thessalonians 5:17)

With that in mind, how significant must prayer be in the edification process for believers to grow up to maturity in Jesus Christ? The Scriptures tell us that God calls upon us to pray – to pray at all times, to pray without ceasing, to pray with thankful hearts, to pray with gladness, to pray instead of worrying, to pray for one another, to pray when we fall. But for the sake of His name in all things...PRAY!

In other words, our commitment to belong to the body of Christ is a commitment to undergird its ministry with prayer. We need to pray in order to cultivate the kind of relationship with the Lord that is needed to make a meaningful contribution to the life of the body. We need the prayers of others who will intercede on our behalf and plead our case with the Father. We need to pray together about matters of mutual concern, kingdom issues that require our combined efforts in prayer.

Yes, the institution called "a church" could get along without prayer, as long as it attempts nothing more than the vain busyness and trivial pursuits of a human agency. But no church that has anything to do with the eternal business of the King of glory should dare to continue without steadfast, fervent, persistent, dynamic prayer. Jesus said, "Apart from Me, you can do nothing," and without prayer, all of our best efforts are just that...nothing!

The prayer life of a congregation will tell as much about the nature of its ministry than perhaps any other single factor can. When the individual and corporate prayer lives of a body of believers grows and stretches with the extension of its reach into the throne room of heaven and the far corners of the earth, God will move His hand to bring blessing upon that people.

Over the years I have come to believe that there are men and women in every congregation of true believers who have a special calling and giftedness in the area of prayer. Make no mistake about it – everyone is called to pray because the nature of our new creaturehood establishes prayer as an integral part of our birthright in Jesus Christ. But every church needs people who have been particularly burdened by the Lord to carry an extra portion of the load for the ministries of the body. Providence has been unusually blessed in that regard since its earliest days. No other explanation accounts for all that the Lord has done in this ministry. People have prayed and God Himself has responded by bringing forth much fruit!

The hardest work I face in any given week is not the steady stream of meetings and counseling sessions, not the problems associated with the administrative affairs of the congregation, not even the difficulties associated with studying the Scriptures, developing sermons, and preaching each Sunday. No, the toughest task before me each day is to enter into the quiet place of prayer and meet the Lord just to talk things over. For some that is hard to imagine since prayer comes so easily for them, but for the rest of us, prayer demands a higher level of discipline and labor than anything else we do. Even as pastors, we often shift prayer to the bottom of our "to do" list, rather than to the place of highest priority.

What if you are not especially comfortable in prayer? You may have trouble spending even the briefest moments in focused prayer because your mind wanders as soon as you utter your first words to the Lord. Concentration comes hard for you, and the song "Sweet Hour of Prayer" seems to be an impossibility given your attention span! Is there hope for you? Can you really make a difference in the life and ministry of your church with your humble efforts in prayer?

You do not have to have any unique calling to grow in your prayer life. God invites you to talk with Him, to listen to His voice, and to respond. He wants you to observe the needs in your life and the lives of others and to tell Him about the desires of your heart. Study His Word to discover what He wants and then agree with Him in times of prayer. Shall His invitation to pray go unheeded? We must not deprive ourselves of such a valued source of power or the comfort and confidence in the One who has promised to hear and answer us when we call upon Him.

Knowing that prayer is so important and yet so easy to neglect, I urge you to make the commitment to stick it out and to prevail in prayer. Armed with this determination, your church will provide the context for others to grow and develop together in the life of prayer and to bring glory to God.

The Ministry of Relationships

Relationships matter. They are important to us, and they are important to God. He even sent His only Son to earth to establish a relationship with us.

The unity of His Church depends upon each member's understanding that we are joined together as joint participants in one body. Fellowship with one another provides mutual support and the opportunity to share ministry and grow together in active, meaningful relationships. This fellowship gives every member a sense of belonging and acceptance among people who really care about them.

How can we broaden and deepen our relationships with one another? Here are the ways the New Testament believers edified one another in their relationships:

- Sharing together in the breaking of bread, both as an act of eating meals together and observing the Lord's Supper (Acts 2:42)

- Encouraging one another (Colossians 2:2-5; Hebrews 10:24-25)

- Giving up personal rights so that the body may be better served and enjoy the unity of the Spirit (Acts 4:32; Ephesians 4:2-3)

- Exhorting and imploring everyone to walk in a manner worthy of our calling (Ephesians 4:1)

- Increasing in love for one another as evidenced by prayer for, and service to, each other (1 Thessalonians 3:10-13)

- Developing the life of the body through the recognition and exercise of each individual's spiritual gifts (Ephesians 4:11-16)

Throughout the New Testament, two Greek words are used again and again to point us in the right direction for a proper appreciation of the value and need for fellowship. *Koinonia* refers to "fellowship, partnership, communion, joint partakers," and *allelon* refers to "one-another" or a commitment to each other in the special fellowship of the body of Christ.

Here are just a few examples of that "one-anotherness":

- "**Be devoted to one another** *in brotherly love;* **give preference to one another** *in honor*" (Romans 12:10)

- "**Be of the same mind toward one another**" (Romans 12:16)

- "*Therefore, laying aside falsehood, speak truth, each one of you, with his neighbor, for* **we are members of one another**" (Ephesians 4:25)

- "*And* **be kind to one another**, *tender-hearted,* **forgiving each other**, *just as God in Christ has also forgiven you*" (Ephesians 4:32)

- "*Let the word of Christ richly dwell within you, with all wisdom teaching and* **admonishing** *one another with psalms and hymns and spiritual songs, singing with thankfulness in your hearts to God*" (Colossians 3:16)

- *"Therefore* **encourage one another***, and* **build up one another***, just as you also are doing"* (1 Thessalonians 5:11)

- *"Beloved, if God so loved us, we also ought to* **love one another** (1 John 4:11)

As growing believers, we all need spiritual fellowship, the kind that encourages relationships promoting godliness and Christlikeness in the way we interact with one another. Where there is godly fellowship, there will be healthy relationships. Where there is no godly fellowship but only friendships with ungodly people, there will be no progress in strong, healthy, spiritually nurturing relationships that build us up in Christ. The relationship we have with Him provides the model for the relationships we have with others in the body of Christ. We love others because He taught us how to love. He did that by loving us unconditionally and giving Himself freely to us just as He expects us to do with one another.

The connection between our love for Him and our love for others appears most clearly in Jesus' treasured words about the two great commandments: "You shall love the Lord your God with all your heart, and with all your soul, and with all your mind....You shall love your neighbor as yourself" (Matthew 22:37, 39).

The Ministry of Instruction

Just as the physical body needs food for nourishment, so the body of Christ needs spiritual food in order to be healthy. That food can be found only in the Word of God as we take in its rich provisions for the growth and edification of our souls. Christians cannot forsake instruction in the Scriptures without seriously jeopardizing their spiritual well-being and compromising the rest of the body through their spiritual anemia. Since the strength and health of the Church depend upon it, we must be committed to the faithful teaching of the Word of God in order that every member may grow in the Lord. This instruction must be thorough and consistent in its preparation and delivery.

A pastor must make it a high priority to devote plenty of time in his regular ministry schedule to study, discuss, apply, explain, refute unsound or false teaching, and provide opportunities for every member to have access to the kind of instruction that not only ministers to the mind, but also to the heart. The Puritan writer, Thomas Brooks, addressed this issue when he wrote:

> "A little knowledge that divinely affects the heart, is infinitely better than a world of that swimming knowledge that swims in the head, but never sinks down into the heart, to the bettering, to the warming, and to the affecting of it. Therefore strive not so much to know, as to have thy heart affected with what thou knowest; for heart-affecting knowledge is the only knowledge that accompanies salvation, that will possess thee of salvation."[1]

How can we edify one another in the ministry of instruction? To be effective, the ministry of instruction in the body of Christ should include the following:

- Teaching and preaching the Word of God, the Bible (Acts 2:42)

- Strengthening the faith of each member through faithful application of the Word (Acts 14:21-22)

- Following up with new believers to see them firmly established in the faith (Acts 15:36)

- Refuting unsound doctrine, false teaching, and vain speculation wherever it appears (1 Timothy 1:3-7)

- Training others to teach the Word also and extend further the message of God's Word (2 Timothy 2:2)

---

1 Thomas Brooks, *The Works of Thomas Brooks, Volume II* (Carlisle, Pennsylvania: The Banner of Truth Trust, 1980) 439.

- Seeking to live holy and blameless lives according to what is taught (1 Peter 1:15-16)

- Holding forth the goal of all instruction: "Love from a pure heart and a good conscience and a sincere faith" (1 Timothy 1:5)

Knowledge for the sake of knowledge has little value for the growth of the individual. Instruction should lead men and women of God to live holy and blameless lives in the power of the Spirit as they learn more of what brings pleasure to the heart of the Lord.

Therefore, all members should seek regular times of instruction in the Word as well as training in how to study the Scriptures for themselves. Without personal interaction with the Scriptures, a grave danger threatens the entire body. Insufficient instruction or a lack of personal Bible study opens the door to the danger of false teaching and unsound doctrines inconsistent with the Word of God.

We are told in Acts 17:11 that the believers in Berea were more noble than those in Thessalonica "for they received the Word with great eagerness, examining the Scriptures daily, to see whether these things were so." Therefore, you must never rely solely on what someone tells you the Bible says. Make it your practice to study the Scriptures yourself in order to make sure that the message you are receiving – and teaching – is true.

Part of the responsibility we have for one another is to see that each of us is trained in knowing how to study and then to teach others what we have learned and are learning from His Word. We must be sure that instruction, teaching, training, and all other means of engrafting the Word into our lives is a primary part of our walk with Christ.

The Word of God cannot "dwell in you richly" if you do not learn to take it in personally and let it satisfy your own soul first, before preparing to give it out (Colossians 3:16). May we heed these instructions from Paul to all believers: "Be diligent to present yourself approved to God as a workman who does not need to be ashamed, handling accurately the word of truth" (2 Timothy 2:15).

When believers think of themselves more highly than they ought to think, they separate themselves from Christ Himself – who came to serve, not to be served.

The Son of Man did not come

to be served, but to serve,

and to give His life a ransom for many.

Matthew 20:28

13

More Keys for Edification

History reveals that the commitment level of the modern church pales in comparison to the church in other ages. Yet the problems we run into today are really no different from those faced by the early church.

We are facing a dilemma that affects educational institutions and the print media as well as the Church. Some have called it "the dumbing down of America" or lowering the standard so that people can succeed not by diligence but by asking less. A cartoon in *Leadership Journal* in 1983[1] showed a sign in front of a church called "The Lite Church." It read:

24% Fewer Commitments
Home of the 7.5% Tithe
15-minute Sermons
45-minute Worship Services
We Have Only 8 Commandments – Your Choice
We Use Just 3 Spiritual Laws and Have an
800-year Millennium
Everything You've Wanted in a Church...and Less!

As the years have gone by, I have seen more indications that people would flock to that kind of congregation because they do not necessarily want more of the Lord – they want fewer demands upon their time and resources.

---

1 This cartoon appeared in the *Leadership Journal* 4 (1983): 81. Artist, Gerry Mooney. Concept, Jim Berkley.

Unfortunately, far too many Christians are willing to accept the benefits of belonging to the body but are not willing to offer themselves in service to the body. One of Providence's core values states that no task should ever be considered beneath any member (see the Core Values of Providence Appendix). Haughty spirits and proud hearts account for much of the pain and broken relationships within the Church. When believers think of themselves more highly than they ought to think, they separate themselves from Christ Himself – who came to serve, not to be served (Romans 12:3; Matthew 20:28).

The Ministry of Service

If a congregation begins to demonstrate a spirit of pride and begins to show preference in the way it treats people, servanthood will be the first casualty. Those unwilling to serve start to look for others who will serve them. Soon, an attitude that elevates one above another develops, and the Church begins to suffer from a deficiency of servants and an ungodly spirit of selfishness among those God called to follow Christ.

How can we discourage this spirit of partiality and encourage the ministry of service in the body of Christ? The Scriptures reveal several areas that should be included in our ministry of service:

- Caring for the poor (Deuteronomy 15:7-11), the elderly (Leviticus 19:32; 1 Timothy 5:3), the sick, the bereaved, the imprisoned, the downtrodden and victims of injustice (Matthew 25:35-40), and the widows and orphans (James 1:27)

- Counseling for the confused, the hurting, the seeking (Proverbs 19:20-21)

- Discipline for the unruly, the ungodly, and the impenitent (Matthew 18:15-20)

- Reconciliation for the estranged – litigations, separations in marriage, disagreements among members (2 Corinthians 5:18-19; 1 Corinthians 6:1-7)

Take a few minutes to consider this question. You may be a pastor, deacon, or Bible study leader, but are you a servant? One sure test is to observe your own response when someone treats you like one! Churches need pastors and members who love serving because they know whatever they do, they do it for the glory of God (1 Corinthians 10:31). Serving at any level brings joy to those who understand their true position in Christ, the One who "emptied Himself, taking the form of a bond-servant" (Philippians 2:7).

The Ministry of Management

God's ownership of all things should be an undisputed fact acknowledged by every believer. The earth and all that is in it belongs to Him. We affirm that truth without question with our mouths, but have difficulty acting as if that were true in how we handle things He entrusts to our care. Perhaps we need to hear once more what the Scriptures say:

> "For by Him all things were created, both in the heavens and on earth, visible and invisible, whether thrones or dominions or rulers or authorities – all things have been created by Him and for Him." (Colossians 1:16)

> "The earth is the LORD's, and all it contains, the world, and those who dwell in it." (Psalm 24:1)

More likely than not, while agreeing that He owns what has come into our hands, we are inclined to function as if the possession of the goods gives us the right to appropriate all things without reference to the intentions of the true owner, God Himself.

Therefore, stewardship or management[2] issues constantly barrage members of the body of Christ as we are forced to deal with the temptation to spend His resources on ourselves. In the process, we are then confronted with the matter of tithing, or returning at least a tenth of what He provides back to Him through the Church. The idea of giving offerings over and above the tithe forces us to expand our understanding of God's ownership, since we want to determine how we will spend the remaining ninety percent.

How can we learn to be better stewards and managers of His resources – and what shall we teach those under our care? A careful study of the Scriptures reveal the following principles:

- We must acknowledge that the ownership of all things belongs to the Lord (Psalm 24:1; 1 Corinthians 10:26).

- We must recognize that every area of life – time (Ephesians 5:15-16), talent (Matthew 25:24f.), and treasure (Matthew 6:21) – should be managed with good principles of stewardship.

- We must expect that every believer will honor the Lord in obedience through faithful gifts of tithes and offerings (Malachi 3:10).

- We must walk with Christ in a manner that maintains balanced priorities among the multiple areas of ministry responsibility in each believer's life (Matthew 6:33).

How, then, will we learn how to live together and grow up together in Christ if we deliberately act irresponsibly and selfishly with the resources

---

2 The Greek word usually translated as "steward" is *oikonomos*, which means "house manager." We are entrusted with the resources of the Lord so that we might function as His managers. Therefore, biblical stewardship as a whole is nothing more, but certainly nothing less, than the management of the possessions of God: "Let a man regard us in this manner, as servants of Christ, and stewards [managers] of the mysteries of God. In this case, moreover, it is required of stewards [managers] that one be found trustworthy" (1 Corinthians 4:1-2).

He has asked us to manage for Him? Stewardship has to do with management. God has called us to manage the time, talents, and treasures He has placed under our supervision. As a show of good faith and an act of obedience, He requires a tithe from each of us, one-tenth of that which comes under our care. All of it belongs to Him, but He will allow us to use some for our own needs if we act with integrity with the portion He requires for Himself.

Good stewardship builds and reveals integrity. Bad stewardship exposes selfish and foolish hearts. We cannot ignore the reality that our response to the practice of good stewardship reveals our heart's preoccupation more than just about any other area of our life in Christ. If He is indeed Lord of all things in our lives, how can we continually mismanage and misappropriate such temporal things like material goods and money? Sadly, one sure way to reveal the actual priorities of our lives is to check our checkbooks and bank accounts. For where our treasure is, there will our hearts be also (Matthew 6:21).

Stewardship plays an important part in the life of the Church, both as a means of providing for ministry needs and as a means of determining the condition of our hearts before the Lord. Our tithes and offerings either mock Him through our defiant and embezzling spirits or honor Him through our obedience. When we learn to do what God expects of every member in the area of stewardship, we bring honor to His Son, Jesus Christ.

The Results of Biblical Edification

Slowly but surely, the ministry of edification does its work as we advance in the maturing process, becoming a little more like Jesus each day.

When we commit ourselves to *prayer*, the Lord faithfully answers our prayers – encouraging our confidence in Him and leading us to know what it means to trust Him more. When we participate in *fellowship* with other believers, we engage in significant and meaningful relationships, causing us to grow in our ability to love others more genuinely and to learn to love

Christ more fully. When we take advantage of the opportunities for biblical *instruction*, we grow in the knowledge of Jesus Christ, which leads us to know Him more personally and intimately. When we *serve* in His name, we grow in our humility before Him and others, leading us to long to imitate Him more. Lastly, when we practice sound *management* (or stewardship), we grow in personal integrity before the Lord, and find that in doing so, we honor Him with our faithfulness and obedience. As we do these things, we grow up to maturity in Christ and make Him known as His life is revealed in us.

The following table identifies the characteristics of Christ built up in us when we practice these biblical means of edification. It also shows how we will respond to Christ as a result of the edification process.

EDIFICATION IN...	BRINGS INCREASED...	AND WE WILL...
Prayer	Confidence	Trust Him more
Relationships	Intimacy	Love Him more
Instruction	Knowledge	Know Him more
Service	Humility	Imitate Him more
Management	Integrity	Honor Him more

Remember the unfinished building project? Praise God that our heavenly Father is committed to finishing the work He has started in us. As all of us contribute to the ministry of edification, we will be made complete in Christ and will work toward presenting every member complete in Christ (Colossians 1:28-29).

The Content of Our Ministry: What We Must Do

We have examined three major areas of emphasis (exaltation, evangelism, and edification) and have noted several points in each area that demand our attention. At Providence, we actually ask every member to be involved in each area. We want membership in a covenant community of faith to mean something! We have no desire to build up massive numbers on our membership rolls – our deepest desire is to welcome men and women of God who will join together in the body of Christ to do what He wants His people to do.

In the previous chapters, we have looked together at the Scriptures to discover the answers to these two questions: What should the content of our ministry be? And what must we do in order to glorify God as the body of Christ?

Now let's look at *how* we are to do it.

Section Three

THE GODLY CHARACTER OF MINISTRY

Being fitted and held together...
according to the proper working
of each individual part.
Ephesians 4:16

God's work cannot be reduced to simple
formulas, developed by well-intentioned
church technicians, that can be packaged,
purchased, and guaranteed to work
in your church.

Oh, the depth of the riches of the wisdom

and knowledge of God! How unsearchable His

judgments, and His paths beyond tracing out!

Romans 11:33 (NIV)

14

Structural Integrity

Architectural structures offer a fascinating insight into the personalities of those who are doing the building. In the late 1990s, a national park completed a public restroom facility on one of its hiking trails that cost somewhere in the neighborhood of $330,000! To make this extravagance even worse, the cost did not even include running water since none was available to pipe in.

I may be a little more frugal than some, but I'm not sure I could justify spending that much money on a structure to be used only occasionally by the dozen or so hikers who happen to pass by. On top of that, it seems that the purpose of the facility does not lend itself to such a costly construction design!

When we build a new structure, it should suit the purpose for which the building is to be used. This philosophy holds true when we think about how we should go about structuring our ministry. How should we do what God has called us to do? Ministry that glorifies the Lord has to take into consideration not only what we do – but how, or in what manner, we do it. What we do focuses on *content;* how we do it focuses on *character.*

We have spent the last several chapters focusing on the content of our ministry and looking at what God wants His Church to be. Now we turn our attention to the character of our ministry and focus on how He wants us to do it.

The structural character of our ministry must be consistent with the spiritual content of our ministry. It simply would not do to have lofty and glorious ministries to pursue, but to work toward accomplishing them in a profane and unworthy manner. We want there to be a match between the character and the content of our ministry.

Much of the ministry going on in churches today has been nullified in its goal to glorify the Lord simply because it violates the integrity of the work of the Holy Spirit in the way it is done. How can the Lord be honored when we serve Him with an unwilling spirit and a resentful heart? Where is the eternal value in giving thousands of dollars to missions when not one word of intercessory prayer accompanies the monetary gift? What message do we send the Lord when we demand a high level of commitment to personal evangelism in our churches but are unwilling to sacrificially invest our own lives in leading someone to Christ? How can a family live for Christ when it is so busy with church activities that there is no time left to build a godly home where righteous and wholesome relationships thrive in both the marriage and with the children?

We can do the right things and do them in the wrong way. Our calling as believers is to discover not only what the Lord wants us to do, but how He wants us to live. He is concerned first with our being and *then* with our doing!

The issues related to the character of our ministry fall into two categories: structural character and spiritual character. In this chapter and the next, we will examine the impact each makes on the ministry God has given us as His Church.

The Structural Character of Ministry

In some organizations, it may make sense to adopt the latest structural flowchart from a Fortune 500 company or to implement trendy business practices, but not when it comes to running a church. As the body of Christ, the structure and means of operation must retain the character of the One who rules sovereignly over His body. Therefore, when we know what we have been called to do (according to our study of the content of our ministry in Chapters 4-13), we must then pursue biblical principles in the way we organize and monitor how we go about our ministry.

How can we structure our ministry so that it is both effective and pleasing to Christ? As always, we look to the Scriptures for answers. Several biblical characteristics will protect our organizational integrity as we minister in the name of Christ. A church that is organized with biblical integrity must be:

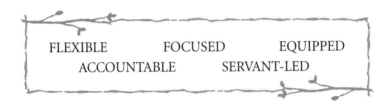

FLEXIBLE   FOCUSED   EQUIPPED
ACCOUNTABLE   SERVANT-LED

Structured for Flexibility

When Jesus spoke of the radical impact the gospel would have in our lives, the need for change was particularly evident in His example of the new wine being placed in old wineskins (Matthew 9:17). If there is insufficient flexibility in the wineskins to handle the growth of the fermented wine, the drastic change would be destructive to both the wine and the wineskin. Likewise, the Church has to be ready and willing to change its structures to accommodate the growth Christ brings in the lives of its members.

In an insightful explanation of this account of new wine and old wineskins, A. B. Bruce,[1] a pastor with the Free Church of Scotland, wrote in 1871:

> "Hence the *vis inertiae* of established custom evermore
> insists on adherence to what is old, till the new wine proves

---

1 A. B. Bruce, *The Training of the Twelve*, 4th ed. (Grand Rapids, Michigan: Kregel Publications, 1971) 76-78.

its power by producing an explosion needlessly wasteful, by which both wine and bottles often perish, and energies which might have quietly wrought out a beneficent reformation are perverted into blind powers of indiscriminate destruction....The same thing happens to a greater or lesser extent every generation; for new wine is always in course of being produced by the eternal vine of truth, demanding in some particulars of belief and practice new bottles for its preservation, and receiving for answer an order to be content with the old ones.

"...It is as if Jesus had said: 'I do not wonder that you love the old wine of Jewish piety, fruit of a very ancient vintage; or even that you dote upon the very bottles which contain it, covered over with the dust and cobwebs of ages. But what then? Do men object to the existence of new wine, or refuse to have it in their possession, because the old is superior in flavor? No: they drink the old, but they carefully preserve the new, knowing that the old will get exhausted, and that the new, however harsh, will mend with age, and may ultimately be superior even in flavor to that which is in present use. Even so should you behave towards the new wine of my kingdom. You may not straightway desire it, because it is strange and novel; but surely you might deal more wisely with it than merely spurn it, or spill and destroy it!'

"Too seldom for the church's good have lovers of old ways understood Christ's wisdom, and lovers of new ways sympathized with His charity."

The changing scene of the Church in the developing world today provides some interesting test cases for how flexible the church should be in allowing the Lord to shape the form new churches will take. For example, in Central Asia, there has been no viable Christian witness for generations because of the oppressive measures taken by communism and the violent dogmatism of radical Islam. With the fall of the Soviet Union in the early 1990s, the doors of opportunity for the gospel were cracked open and now the number of Christians in the region is increasing.

What will "church" look like when these new believers begin to assemble to fulfill their biblical calling to congregate under Christ's headship? Will it be patterned after the Protestant or Roman Catholic churches of the West, the Orthodox traditions of the East, the state church traditions, or some other model? Without understanding the importance of flexibility, church leaders could do irreparable damage to the effectiveness of emerging churches if they impose an awkward, foreign model on these brand-new churches among new believers.

Noted Christian leader and author Howard Hendricks once said, "The church must learn to distinguish between the unchangeable and what must be changed."[2] But sadly, many American believers could not function in churches where following Christ did not retain their established traditions and habits of congregating. We need to develop and maintain structures that hold onto biblical essentials while allowing maximum flexibility in nonessential areas. The Bible, not our traditions, enables us to determine what is essential and what is not. In order for the ministry to develop flexibility, it must be innovative and affirm the diversity of the body of Christ.

A Flexible Structure Must Be Innovative

Flexibility allows us to look to the Lord for new and fresh ways to organize and structure ourselves for effective ministry. That which is tried and true may work most of the time under certain circumstances, but we need to be alert to different ways and fresh insights about how to engage in ministry. Every present-day tradition started out at one time as an innovation; the Church has not always functioned as it has now nor will it continue to function that way in the future.

According to many students of church history and the state of the Church, during the 1990s decisive shifts occurred in the culture of the

2 Stated during a message to the congregation of Providence Baptist Church on March 22, 1998.

Church toward new approaches to ministry, including new music styles, multimedia presentations, and even new codes of dress. Rather than be threatening, innovation should encourage believers to look for ways to improve and grow in their persistent endeavors to "excel still more" (1 Thessalonians 4:1).

A Flexible Structure Must Be Diverse

Since we are not all alike, it makes sense that our diversity would keep us from falling into the trap of thinking that God has called the Church to adopt a "one-size-fits-all" mentality regarding ministry structure. The needs of people are as diverse as the people themselves. The structure of our ministry must be flexible enough to change as it needs to so that folks with diverse needs, distinctive backgrounds, unique circumstances, and other differences too numerous to count might come and meet Christ in a personal, meaningful way.

Structured to Be Focused

Since the latter half of the twentieth century, the Lord has been moving in exciting ways in the Church around the world. Stories of revival, renewal, and great increases in the number who are responding to the gospel abound. As a result, trend-watchers have been working to discover common methods that could be reproducible in churches in other parts of the world. Although I am certain that some common techniques exist, I am even more certain of two things: 1) the Lord's hand is responsible for anything good that is happening; and 2) nearly everything else is different! In other words, the Lord seldom does things the same. His ways are often inscrutable. Although His methods are unpredictable, He never ceases to work among His people to bring glory to His name. We simply cannot expect God to pass on to us a single blueprint as His grand architectural design for the effective church.

Why? Too much evidence exists to support His delight in diversity. God's work cannot be reduced to simple formulas, developed by well-intentioned church technicians, that can be packaged, purchased, and guaranteed to work in your church. Trends in churches around America entice many to try to do everything that every other church is doing anywhere that it seems to be working. Pastors and congregations jump on one bandwagon after another, so they will not miss something that might be good. If that actually worked, then the best way to build a strong church would be to take the top twenty or so churches in the country and try to imitate everything each one of them is doing. That is impossible and should never be tried!

God authored all the different ministry styles, ordered the distinctive priorities of individual congregations, and gifted various churches with unique qualities. I believe that He is grieved when He sees churches losing their specific focus on what He has called them to do in ministry. Many churches have been captivated by seductive philosophies and have been enticed to leave their first love. Granted there are those who unknowingly have been used by the enemies of Christ to distract the Church. Some have even resorted to deceptive practices and worldly power games to try to get their way. Paul warned the church at Ephesus that this would happen, so we have no reason to be surprised (Ephesians 4:14). However, we do have reason to focus more strongly on the race we have been called to run.

Yet there will always be those who want to become a part of a church in order to remake it in the image of the one they just left. Their call to ministry as they understand it is to see how quickly they can conform the ministry of their new church into the other one. If the leadership and congregation in our church attempted such foolishness by responding to every alternative with which we have been presented, the church would have died long ago, and we would have exhausted each other in the process!

The only acceptable solution is to stay on target and pour our lives into the unique ministry calling God has given to each congregation. As a pastor, you and your leaders must determine what your primary objectives are and keep them before your flock. Continue to press forward on the most direct course of action so that you will not be steered away from the path God has laid out for your church. As a member, you must recognize that not all churches are called by God to do and be the same thing. Some are structured for urban ministry; some are not. Some are called to establish a Christian school; some are not. In every case, we must recognize that God has called each body to focus on some facet of His work that is unique to them.

Structured for Equipping

Too many Christians have identified success in ministry as getting large numbers of believers together. Rallying the troops to assemble has become more significant than the battle we are assembling for. Proponents of more sophisticated and more frequent gatherings perpetuate the idea that the meeting is the main event; they don't understand that gathering together is only a means toward the end of scattering into the world as better equipped ministers of the gospel than we were before.

Our conviction that we must take the message of God's Kingdom into the world dictates that we disperse each week, representing Jesus Christ and His Church wherever we happen to go and whatever we happen to do. This ministry strategy calls for each member to be prepared, equipped, and then scattered abroad in Jesus' name.

Therefore, I encourage you to organize ministries around those things that will maximize your efforts to train and prepare people to put their training into action. The world is filled with searching people who need answers from those who are equipped to provide them. We cannot spend all our time in gatherings, nor in training, nor in planning. If we are so busy figuring out how to go to more meetings, more study groups, and more training seminars, we will never get around to ministry.

We have an obligation to one another to resist lifestyles and ministry structures that fill up our lives with busywork for Jesus. Each meeting, each study, each time together should contribute toward the accomplishment of some aspect of what God has called us to do as individuals and as a church. Being equipped is not the end God has in mind for us, but rather being equipped so we might *serve Him* fully is what He has in mind. We have been *gathered* that we might be more effectively *scattered*!

Structured to Be Accountable

When I was in high school, I lived in the city of Graham, North Carolina, population 8,000. Nearly everyone in town knew everyone else, or so it seemed. Therefore, it was not that surprising when one afternoon my mom called me from her job at City Hall to tell me the chief of police wanted to see me.

Not knowing what he could possibly want, I went to the police station where I was questioned about an incident the previous evening in which the town water tower had been painted. There, in giant letters visible for several miles, someone had painted "DH, 1970"– my initials and the year I was to graduate from high school. After assuring the police that I had nothing to do with it (seriously, I didn't!), it dawned on me that there was little you could get away with in a small town. Someone was always there to hold you accountable.

In previous eras of church history, members of the body of Christ were held to a high standard of expectations as they shared a mutual accountability with each other. Moral and ethical behavior was assumed to be under the watchful eye of the church, and members knew that what they did was informally and lovingly monitored by other church members. It was important that the testimony of the entire congregation not be smeared by the actions of a few.

Unfortunately, cultural changes have advocated tolerance as a higher value than righteousness, and the Church has followed suit. We dare not raise an accusation or even imply wrongdoing anymore lest we be subjected to charges of narrow judgmentalism. Accountability had all but disappeared until just a few years ago when the Church began to wake up to the steady slide of its members into ungodliness and a general laxity about purity and holiness.

But instead of providing a context for accountability, churches are often structured so that no one is closely connected to anyone who cares enough to confront unbiblical and un-Christlike lifestyles and choices. Some have even suggested that the size of the church determines whether there is any practical accountability. In reality, every church – no matter the size – can provide a safe haven in which people can hide their blind spots, protect their secret sins, and seclude themselves in relative anonymity.

Accountable Through Small Group Structure

We should structure ourselves so that everyone can be a part of a small group of believers who will encourage accountability in our lives. Small group structures provide every member with a place for connecting with other believers in relationships that offer personal, individual encouragement and a trust factor that allows for confidential confession of sins.

We have a responsibility to encourage one another to stand firm in the faith, to grow to maturity in Christ, and to live up to the name we bear as the body of Christ. Paul wrote the following about this responsibility:

> "*Therefore encourage one another, and build up one another, just as you also are doing....And we urge you, brethren, admonish the unruly, encourage the fainthearted, help the weak, be patient with all men.*" (*1 Thessalonians 5:11, 14*)

Paul lays out a plan to hold one another accountable and calls on us to build each other up with the following:

• Encouragement for the fainthearted, the timid

- Warnings to the unruly, disorderly, irresponsible, undisciplined, those who avoid their obligations[3]

- Help and support for the weak

- Patience with everyone

We are not just accountable *to* others, but accountable *for* others so that they might press on in their walk with Christ. We need to look out for each other and leave no one behind! Without the close fellowship that comes within a smaller group, this type of accountability would be totally unrealistic.

But there is another benefit to be gained in building fellowship and accountability together. Besides just the accountability context of small groups, the relationships developed open doors for trust and confidentiality among people who genuinely care about each other's spiritual lives. Biblical accountability seeks to offer a means by which believers can confess their sins to one another and know that their confidant is trustworthy. As a result, we can understand the benefit from these instructions given by James: "Confess your sins to one another and pray for one another so that you may be healed" (James 5:16).

Dietrich Bonhoeffer,[4] a German pastor executed near the end of World War II by Hitler's Third Reich, believed in the importance of accountability. He wrote these words on the place of mutual confession of sins among brothers in Christ:

> "A man who confesses his sins in the presence of a brother knows that he is no longer alone with himself; he experiences the presence of God in the reality of the other person. As long as I am by myself in the confessions of my

---

3 "Brethren, even if a man is caught in any trespass, you who are spiritual, restore such a one in a spirit of gentleness; each one looking to yourself, lest you too be tempted" (Galatians 6:1).
4 Dietrich Bonhoeffer, *Life Together* (New York: Harper & Row, 1954) 116.

sins everything remains in the dark, but in the presence of a brother the sin has to be brought into the light. But since the sin must come to light some time, it is better that it happens today between me and my brother, rather than on the last day in the piercing light of the final judgment. It is a mercy that we can confess our sins to a brother. Such grace spares us the terrors of the last judgment."

This in no way suggests that our sin cannot be forgiven by Christ alone, but simply serves as a reminder that God has provided a means by which the forgiveness of Christ can be affirmed by others in the body of Christ. We need the kind of structural character in our ministry that fosters vulnerable, honest relationships within small groups of believers, sharing life together so that no one is ever in isolation.

Accountable Through Every-Member-Ministry Structure

My first driving attempts as an excited 16-year-old were frustrated by the fact that I was behind the wheel of a 1949 Willys Jeep station wagon. Not only was this vintage vehicle without an automatic transmission, but the shift from first to second gear required "double clutching" (pushing in the clutch to get out of first gear and then pushing it in again to get into second). The coordination needed for this action did not come quickly, resulting in loud, grinding noises as the gears tried to engage to keep things moving. This always led to amused stares from passersby!

When gears do not engage, the car will not move. The same thing can be said of the Church. When the members of the body of Christ are not engaged, the ministry does not move. God calls each of us to engage with one another so that the gears of ministry mesh smoothly and the progress of ministry moves effectively.

All of us must do our fair share in shouldering the ministry responsibilities inherent in the body of Christ. It is regrettable to realize that some would presume upon others to do what they are unwilling to do. Then they refuse to be accountable to those who call upon them to do their part! Yet this is true in nearly every church. Instilling in the minds of each member that all are accountable is essential before we can expect everyone to provide "that which every joint supplies according to the proper working of each individual part for the building up of itself in love" (Ephesians 4:16).

We are called to a shared ministry. Once we understand that every member has a ministry, we can move forward in communicating the value of a shared vision for ministry. Each member owes every other member a debt of love, but also a debt of responsibility to understand and to take ownership of the vision God has given to the entire body. We should maintain a high level of accountability to one another as we pursue a shared purpose, shared goals, and shared core values. When we begin to drift from our calling, we need to be held accountable to God's best course for us.

Have you noticed that far too many churches tend to drift off course over the years? The primary reason is that there is no accountability to the vision God has given and soon a change of direction (often imperceptible at first) occurs.

To be engaged in ministry at a level that includes every one of us means that we get the right gears in the right places so that they can work together smoothly. Grinding the gears occurs when we try to mesh with one another while moving in different directions. As noisy as my old jeep was when trying to get from first to second gear, you can only imagine how awful the sound was when I accidentally moved toward reverse instead! Moving harmoniously together necessitates a unified working of the gears so that each plays its part, large or small. So it is for each of us to fulfill our tasks of ministry. We must agree together on where we are heading and how we plan to get there so that a genuine unity of purpose draws and keeps us together.

Structured to Be Servant-led

Leadership in the body of Christ always depends upon the presence of a servant's heart, both in those who lead and in those who are led. If this is missing in either group, ill will and disunity will exist among the people. Self-serving leaders generate an oppressive spirit and resentment among those whom they manipulate for their own satisfaction and control. Self-serving followers chafe and rebel at the slightest provocation and often complain and groan at any evidence that they have not been heard or that their influence has had no impact.

Therefore, a biblical structure for leadership is needed to preserve the character of our ministry. In order for that to take place, two criteria must coexist in the body: leaders who are humble servants and people who are gracious followers.

Churches must understand the critical importance of servant leadership and how fundamental humility of heart and mind are to a leader. If they don't, nothing but trouble will plague them. By violating God's design for what undershepherds must be, many churches have fallen onto hard times and have not been able to recognize the cause of their dilemma. How could it be otherwise? This most basic structural building block cannot be neglected without endangering the spiritual vitality and health of a congregation.

Leaders Must Be Selected for Their Godly Character

Our tendency is to the follow the world's example of selecting leaders with characteristics that make them largely unsuitable for leadership in the Church. God's criteria for His leaders always begin with their Christlike character, not their human ability.

In his profound book, *Spiritual Leadership*, Oswald Sanders[5] offers this helpful and concise comparison of natural leadership and spiritual leadership:

---

5 Oswald Sanders, *Spiritual Leadership* 2nd ed. (Chicago: Moody Press, 1994) 29.

Natural Leader	vs	Spiritual Leader
Self-confident	vs	Confident in God
Knows men	vs	Also knows God
Makes own decisions	vs	Seeks God's will
Ambitious	vs	Self-effacing
Originates own methods	vs	Finds and follows God's methods
Enjoys commanding others	vs	Delights to obey God
Motivated by personal considerations	vs	Motivated by love for God and man
Independent	vs	God-dependent

If we ever substitute natural leadership for spiritual leadership, the ministry of the church will be doomed![6]

Leaders Must Model Leadership with a Servant's Heart

Leaders are best identified by their willingness to serve others and for the model they provide for the congregation to follow. Peter offered the following instructions to elders about this awesome responsibility: "Shepherd the flock of God among you, exercising oversight...not for sordid gain, but with eagerness; nor yet as lording it over those allotted to your charge, but proving to be examples to the flock" (1 Peter 5:2-3).

Without this example of humble servanthood among the leaders, the trickle-down effect will infect the followers with the same kind of haughty spirit they detect in their leaders. Leaders must model servanthood if the Church desires to walk humbly before God.

Biblically qualified leaders have to function within the context of a team of people who are modest about their charge, humbled by their

---

6 A list of those characteristics can be found in 1 Timothy 3:1-13 and Titus 1:5-9.

responsibility, and gracious about their role. Working together with others of like mind and heart, leaders should provide the kind of service to the body of Christ that positions members to be spiritually victorious, for they follow those who follow Christ.

Churches Need Servants Who Follow Graciously

What a pleasant place of ministry belongs to leaders who serve those who know how to follow graciously. Their sweet yieldedness is characteristic of those who are fully surrendered to Christ. Yet leaders cannot expect from their followers what they have not demonstrated. Following when you are used to leading is never easy, but truly godly leaders can never qualify for that role until they have first learned to be gracious followers. When both the leaders and the followers understand humble servanthood, the unity of the body will bear witness to the marvelous presence of Christ in a unique way.

Paul was concerned about this special relationship that must develop between leaders and followers, and he gave instructions to different churches regarding the proper role of both. Perhaps his sensitivity to the heavy weight of ministry among the leaders prompted this word to the church at Thessalonica:

> *"But we request of you, brethren, that you appreciate those who diligently labor among you, and have charge over you in the Lord and give you instruction, and that you esteem them very highly in love because of their work. Live in peace with one another."* (1 Thessalonians 5:12-13)

I have often heard war stories from other pastors, elders, deacons, and church members about the heated battles over power and control within the church, and I know how blessed I have been here at Providence. I am both delighted and amazed at how beautifully God's design works when the right people are in the right positions, serving Christ and His Church with the right attitude.

When the congregation willingly defers to trustworthy leaders who are humbly following Christ, there can be delight in ministry. If God raises up trustworthy leaders in a church, His people will take note and follow them. If these leaders forfeit their right to lead by their failure to be trustworthy before the Lord, the church has a responsibility to hold them accountable. In this event, Paul offers this counsel: "Do not receive an accusation against an elder except on the basis of two or three witnesses. Those who continue in sin, rebuke in the presence of all, so that the rest also may be fearful of sinning" (1 Timothy 5:19-20). If there is no accusation, the body can defer to their leadership with gladness so that they might serve the Lord with gladness, knowing He ultimately holds them accountable (Hebrews 13:17).

As members of the body of Christ, we must pray faithfully for godly wisdom and Christlike character in the leadership of the body. This is just as important as the need for a submissive, yielded spirit among the followers. Too often when disagreements arise, people will *prey* upon their leaders instead of choosing to *pray* for them. Pray for those in leadership to be humble servants who display a shepherd's heart for those allotted to their charge. What a joy it is to serve Christ among a people who pray for their leaders without ceasing, express appreciation graciously, and follow faithfully.

In summary, God wants us to understand that *how* we do things matters just as much to Him as *what* we do. Therefore, as a pastor, be committed to organizing and structuring your church in such a way that in all things Christ is glorified. As a member, commit yourself to servant leadership in your area of ministry and to following your God-given leaders graciously. Let each of us be flexible, focused, equipped, accountable, and servant-led as we help shape the structural character of our ministry. We want to be vessels worthy of carrying the treasure of the gospel and bearing the glory of Christ:

> *"Now in a large house there are not only gold and silver vessels, but also vessels of wood and of earthenware, and*

some to honor and some to dishonor. Therefore, if a man cleanses himself from these things, he will be a vessel for honor, sanctified, useful to the Master, prepared for every good work." (2 Timothy 2:20-21)

In all that we do, and in the way that we do it, may we be vessels of honor for Christ!

To the casual observer, we can appear to be operating at peak efficiency with everything in order, but in fact we may only be holding onto a form of godliness void of the substance and power of godly character.

I know your deeds,

that you have a name that you are alive,

but you are dead.

Revelation 3:1

15

Spiritual Integrity

Someone once said, "Reputation is what you appear to be, but character is what you are when no one is looking!" While most of us want to have a good reputation, from God's perspective it is more important to have a godly character.

Strange as it may seem, many are willing to go to great extremes to guard their reputation but think very little of their character. They care so much about what others think that they lose sight of what God thinks. In the Church, we find that appearances are just as important to people as they are in the secular world. People are usually very concerned about their spiritual reputation, not wanting to risk giving the impression that they are not wise, mature, Christlike, dynamic people.

Yet we all know that from God's point of view, what we want others to think does very little to impress Him. We may say all the right things, show up in all the right places, get involved in doing the right activities, and even dress up in all the right clothing but still lack the only thing that truly matters – being what God wants us to be.

When the New International Version was first published, one of the first editions I owned made a distinct impression on me as I was reading Revelation 3:1. At the bottom of one page were these words from this passage: *"I know your deeds; you have a reputation of being alive...."* Then I turned the page, only to find the words, *"...but you are dead."*

For some reason, this came at a time in my life when I was quite proud of myself and the progress I thought I was making as a Christian. People were beginning to look up to me and to seek my advice. In my mind at least, I had a reputation of being alive but the Lord knew better. He knew that I was a hypocrite hiding behind a mask of outward appearances and that my heart did not fully belong to Him.

In the same way, we can organize the ministry of our churches solely by the structural character issues noted in the previous chapter. To the casual observer, we can appear to be operating at peak efficiency with everything in order, but in fact we may only be holding onto a form of godliness void of the substance and power of godly character (2 Timothy 3:5). In other words, the structure could be a perfectly crafted shell on the outside with nothing living inside.

How then do we avoid the inherent danger of falling into this trap? How do we steer clear of becoming a church with only outward signs of life, measurable though they may be by objective standards? What will keep us fresh and alive, devoted to Christ above all things? If the tangible criteria that are observable are not enough to preserve our spiritual integrity and vitality, what will?

The Spiritual Character of Ministry

The measure of a church's character and its effectiveness in fulfilling its purpose of glorifying God can only be found in the spiritual character of its members. Are they more like Jesus Christ with each passing day? Are their lives more conformed to the image of His Son? Are they yielding positive fruit in their walk with Him (Romans 8:29)?

These questions and a myriad of others frustrate those who want to quantify results and evaluate with total objectivity how the Church is doing.

Yet we know that a church can state its purpose correctly, define the content of its ministry biblically, structure the organization sensitively, and still bear no noticeable resemblance to the character of Christ, its living Head (Ephesians 4:15). We are to grow up in all aspects into Christ and that growth often defies objective measurement. Therefore, we must agree together on certain qualities of godly living that hold out a standard of true spirituality. This brings us to consider the spiritual character of our ministry, an area hard to assess in definitive terms but crucial for a church to bring pleasure to the heart of God.

Five Evidences of Spiritual Growth

It is the Father's desire that His Church be conformed to the image of His Son, but how can we reduce such a lofty goal to a few worthy characteristics to model? Only the naive would believe that the five characteristics described in this chapter represent the full measure of maturity in Christ. However, these characteristics do work to our advantage in that each becomes multidimensional when it finds expression in our lives. Like the fruit of the Spirit described in Galatians 5:22-23, each grows together as a cluster, one reinforcing the other.

As we engage in ministry, regardless of how effective or efficient we are, if these characteristics are not evident in the way we do what we do, we will have failed in our ministry. As we look to Christ and witness the revelation of His glory, we are called to reflect that glory in how we live as members of His body.

We are set apart by Him to be...

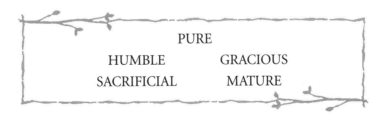

PURE

HUMBLE   GRACIOUS

SACRIFICIAL   MATURE

How do these five evidences of spiritual character affect Christian maturity?

The Evidence of Purity

For Christ to be evident in the Church, how can we be anything less than pure? He has made it clear that because He is holy and righteous, we shall be also: "But like the Holy One who called you, be holy yourselves also in all your behavior; because it is written, "YOU SHALL BE HOLY, FOR I AM HOLY" (1 Peter 1:15-16). Holiness is a difficult concept to imagine since we have so few points of reference outside of Christ by which it can be understood. The word "pure" was chosen here to represent the broader concepts of holiness and righteousness.

What images come to mind when you think of the word "pure"? Several pictures emerge, each offering its own insight into the power of purity as a worthy goal.

Pure as the Driven Snow

Picture in your mind the morning after a heavy snowfall. A vast, soft blanket of white covers everything, making even an ugly eyesore beautiful for a while. We know that we all have sinned, but by the grace of Jesus Christ we can see each other as He does, blanketed with the purifying covering of His redeeming blood. Isaiah expanded our understanding of the impact of purification from sin when he wrote, "Come now, and let us reason together," says the LORD, "Though your sins are as scarlet, they will be as white as snow" (Isaiah 1:18).

Pure as a Virgin

At a wedding not too long ago, the bride asked me to mention during my marriage sermon that she was a virgin and had kept herself sexually pure for this day for her husband. Several young women attending the wedding had been discipled by this special bride, and she wanted to make sure that they all knew that virginity and purity were not old-fashioned, obsolete values, but an appropriate expectation for all who belong to Christ.

We must never take the adoration, affection, and intimacy intended for and due to Christ and give them to another, the way an unfaithful partner would. The Church is betrothed to Christ and must never give away the devotion that is rightfully His through any aspect of its ministry: "For I am jealous for you with a godly jealousy; for I betrothed you to one husband, that to Christ I might present you as a pure virgin" (2 Corinthians 11:2).

Pure Gold

When people speak of something that is unusually valuable to them, they sometimes say that it is pure as gold. Pure gold is totally free from impurity because the fires of the refining process consume all the dross. In Revelation 21:18, John tells us that the Holy City will be made of pure gold – so pure that it will be as transparent as clear glass.

We must learn to welcome the Refiner's fire, which burns away every element of impurity, every evidence of unbelief, every encroachment of mixed devotion. Rather than running from every difficulty and seeing every hardship as punishment, we must understand that God wants to purify and refine us so we will brilliantly reflect His character. He wants to present us as a pure Bride to His Son, Jesus.

Therefore, with these images of purity in mind, can you see how appropriate it is for the character of our ministry to match the purity of Jesus Christ Himself? Peter told us, "Since you have purified your souls in obeying the truth through the Spirit in sincere love of the brethren, love one another fervently with a pure heart" (1 Peter 1:22 NKJV).

The Evidence of Humility

We must be humble men and women of God if we are to become what He calls us to be. Who is better qualified to speak to this point than Peter, the disciple least likely to be nominated as "most humble" among the Twelve? After finding himself completely humiliated by his prideful spirit, Peter was grateful to be restored when Jesus came to him after the resurrection. Listen to the warning tone of Peter's words, words of painful experience, when he wrote to the believers in Asia Minor: "Humble yourselves, therefore, under the mighty hand of God, that He may exalt you at the proper time" (1 Peter 5:6).

If we persist in believing that we have the right to exalt ourselves, we will continue to miss God's intention to exalt us at the proper time. Self-exaltation nullifies the plan of the Lord to bring us to Himself with hearts depending entirely upon Him. Peter learned this lesson only after an agonizing and devastating experience of independent action. The only way to avoid his failure is to avoid his foolish and misplaced confidence in his own ability. To be effective in ministry, we must humble ourselves before the Lord and learn to rely upon Him with an honest estimation of who we really are. We can also humble ourselves knowing that in doing so we follow Christ's example:

> *"Have this attitude in yourselves which was also in Christ Jesus, who, although He existed in the form of God, did not regard equality with God a thing to be grasped, but emptied Himself, taking the form of a bond-servant, and being made in the likeness of men. And being found in appearance as a man, He **humbled Himself** by becoming obedient to the point of death, even death on a cross." (Philippians 2:5-8)*

Without a humble spirit, we will never cultivate a ministry with honest accountability or genuine servant-leaders (characteristics we discussed in the previous chapter on structural character). Our pride will not allow it! We will resist accountability as intrusive and unnecessary meddling rather than welcome it as the preventive and protective measure it is to those who can admit their need.

Leadership – servant leadership in particular – can cause us to chafe with a rebellious spirit and assert our personal autonomy at the expense of living under biblical authority. Our relationships with each other and with the Lord must be shaped by our understanding that we belong to Jesus Christ, we have been bought with the price He paid at the cross, and we are not our own anymore. Therefore, the life of each member of the body must be characterized by humility before God and before each other.

Pride longs to control, to prevail, to have its own way. Unfortunately many of us have enjoyed too much success for our own good and cannot tolerate it when life does not go our way. Yet we will fail to accomplish anything worthwhile in our ministry together if we try to dominate each other or establish boundaries around what God is allowed to touch in our lives.

As the prophet Micah wrote:

> *"He has told you, O man, what is good; and what does the LORD require of you but to do justice, to love kindness, and* ***to walk humbly*** *with your God?" (6:8)*

The Evidence of Graciousness

On any given Sunday, many of us who have spoken or sung of God's grace during the church service will deny that grace before we even leave the building. Does that statement surprise you? We undo the ministry of the Word of God when we talk about others, criticize the worship time, harbor unforgiveness toward someone, or speak unkindly of or to another. Like the seed being snatched away from the rocky soil, ungracious Christians undo the truth of God's grace before it can take root in those who desperately need to know of His unconditional love. How can we avoid such ungracious actions and attitudes? We must remember that grace...

- precludes gossip;

- prevents indifference to the needs of others;

- prevails over critical spirits and judgmental attitudes; and

- pulls our lofty opinions of ourselves down to reality as we understand all that God's grace accomplished on our behalf in Christ Jesus.

We have a responsibility to allow others to see the grace of Christ in us. When we love one another the way Christ does, for example, it soon becomes obvious that that kind of love exceeds any of our individual capabilities. Consequently, we need to seek His empowering grace and then immediately pass it on to others. The very ones who do not deserve it are most likely the ones Jesus will ask us to share it with first!

Hear these words from the Scriptures:

> *"With all humility and gentleness, with patience, showing forbearance for one another in love." (Ephesians 4:2)*

> *"And God is able to make **all grace abound to you,** that always having all sufficiency in everything, you may have an abundance for every good deed." (2 Corinthians 9:8)*

When we refuse to demonstrate a gracious spirit, we lose the opportunity to show others the joy of Christ's love. We also miss the full sufficiency of His abundant grace for everything. Is it not true that our inability to be gracious to others is often directly related to our inability to receive the grace and love Christ offers to us? It is impossible to give away what you do not have. Once the grace of our Lord grips our hearts, how can we dare be anything other than wholly gracious to others?

As Christians, we are the only living link many people have to the loving grace of Jesus Christ. Upon careful observation, can others honestly see Jesus in your congregation? They can, and they will, if the body of believers is made up of one gracious Christian after another.

The Evidence of Sacrifice

Is there any word less descriptive of today's typical American church than "sacrificial"? In Western culture, the emphasis on self-indulgence and the absence of models of self-denial have invaded the Church in such a radical way that the disparity between the pages of the New Testament and the pews of the average congregation could not be greater.

While the need for sacrifice is as great as ever, the character of many believers seems unaffected by the criteria Christ Himself established for His disciples: "If anyone wishes to come after Me, let him deny himself, and take up his cross daily, and follow Me" (Luke 9:23).

For example, an overwhelming percentage of the material wealth available to the Church rests in the hands of Christians in the United States. Yet so little of this wealth makes it back into circulation to accomplish the purposes of Christ. Small congregations in Third World countries struggle to find the means to construct so much as a roof over their heads, while we concern ourselves with whatever level of opulence we can justify in our church facilities. Sacrifice for typical American churchgoers consists of how far we are willing to walk from the paved parking lots (where we have parked our latest model cars) to the church building.

This absence of sacrifice is not limited only to material issues. In some parts of the world, congregations begin to assemble for worship hours before the actual meeting times in order to find a place to sit. But in America, we must frequently contend with church "consumers," who regularly register their displeasure if anything valuable takes place in the first part of the worship service since they habitually arrive well past the starting time.

Even the times scheduled for the services have to take into consideration the unwillingness of many to accept hours inconvenient for them. Any suggestion that people make sacrifices for the greater good of the body of Christ falls on deaf ears.

When assessing the genuine spiritual character of a church, one of the clearest tests of its devotion to Christ can be found in the presence (or absence!) of a sacrificial spirit among its members. This may be evident in the way people care about each other without regard for themselves, or in the way they volunteer to serve even when they know they will gain nothing in return. They may give up their rights to what they want in order to give themselves to purposes that matter. A true spirit of sacrifice will set a people apart from the world as those among whom Christ is at work.

He who sacrificed His life for us calls us to deny ourselves daily and to give ourselves sacrificially for Him and for those He loves. We need to learn to say "no" to ourselves so that the call of Christ is not muffled by the relentless demands to please ourselves. Although it goes against the grain of both our nature and our cultural conditioning, we need to learn to say with Paul,

> *"But whatever things were gain to me, those things I have counted as loss for the sake of Christ. More than that, I count all things to be loss in view of the surpassing value of knowing Christ Jesus my Lord, for whom I have suffered the loss of all things, and count them but rubbish so that I may gain Christ." (Philippians 3:7-8 NASB)*

The Evidence of Maturity

The picture of a little girl with bright red lipstick on, dressed up in her mother's old dress, wearing her high heel shoes, and carrying a huge purse comes to mind when I try to imagine how we must look to God when we try to pretend we are already mature. We want so badly to be mature that we work hard to give every appearance of maturity. Yet the fact remains that the Lord's definition of maturity is the only one that matters – regardless of how much we want to project the image of those who have already reached the goal.

"When I was a child, I used to speak as a child, think as a child, reason as a child; when I became a man, I did away with childish things" (1 Corinthians 13:11). Paul's words remind us that as we grow up, childish living loses its charm and maturity must take the place of immaturity.

Paul also speaks of our need to be innocent and childlike with regard to evil, but seasoned and mature in our thinking: "Brethren, do not be children in your thinking; yet in evil be babes, but in your thinking be mature" (1 Corinthians 14:20). We are to be mature men and women of God in our thoughts, actions, emotional responses, relationships, decision-making, understanding of the things of God, and in a host of other ways.

The character of Christ will be evident in us as we mature in Him, are conformed to His likeness, and grow up in all respects to be like Him. The good news is that we have no reason to settle for less than His standard. Our Lord has committed all the authority and resources of His own power to conform us to the image of His Son. This expectation is outlined in many places throughout the Scriptures.

Here are just a few passages that highlight just how important maturity is to the Lord:

> "Until we all attain to the unity of the faith, and of the knowledge of the Son of God, to a mature man, to the measure of the stature which belongs to the fullness of Christ. As a result, we are **no longer to be children,** tossed here and there by waves and carried about by every wind of doctrine, by the trickery of men, by craftiness in deceitful scheming; but speaking the truth in love, we are to grow up in all aspects into Him who is the head, even Christ, from whom the whole body, being fitted and held together by what every joint supplies, according to the proper working of each individual part, causes the growth of the body for the building up of itself in love." (Ephesians 4:13-16 NASB)

> "God willed to make known [to you] what is the riches of the glory of this mystery among the Gentiles, which is Christ in you, the hope of glory. And we proclaim Him, admonishing every man and teaching every man with all wisdom, that we may present every man **complete in Christ**." (Colossians 1:27-28)

> "Beloved, now we are children of God, and it has not appeared as yet what we shall be. We know that, when He

appears, we **shall be like Him,** *because we shall see Him just as He is. And everyone who has this hope fixed on Him purifies himself, just as He is pure." (1 John 3:2-3)*

"For though by this time you ought to be teachers, you have need again for someone to teach you the elementary principles of the oracles of God, and you have come to need milk and not solid food....But solid food is **for the mature,** *who because of practice have their senses trained to discern good and evil....Therefore leaving the elementary teaching about the Christ, let us* **press on to maturity,** *not laying again a foundation of repentance from dead works and of faith toward God." (Hebrews 5:12, 14, 6:1)*

Is there any question, then, that God wants us to grow up and become men and women of mature character? Our ultimate ministry goal is to see each person become complete in Christ, demonstrating His character and reflecting His image in every possible way. That will be evident in the maturity of our worship, the maturity of our service, the maturity of our relationships, the maturity of our response to hard times, the maturity of our knowledge (manifested in godly wisdom and discernment), and in a multitude of other ways.

I'll admit that it is much easier to measure quantity in our ministry by the number of people, dollars, and square feet that can be accumulated and accounted for. Yet the quality – or the spiritual character – of ministry deals with the kinds of subjective traits only the Lord can track. We have stopped short of our calling if we become satisfied with the outward trappings of ministry success and neglect the inward track of spiritual growth.

The spiritual character of our ministry matters even more than its structural character. Therefore, let us resist the temptation to measure ourselves by objective standards alone and focus instead on Christ Himself, proclaiming Him in order that we present everyone complete in Christ (Colossians 1:28).

A bridegroom would never forget the
insensitivity and carelessness of an unkempt
bride who did not bother to prepare for her
wedding day. Why do we think that we can
approach Christ as His Bride with so little
interest in becoming all that He desires?

Let us rejoice and be glad and give the glory

to Him, for...His bride has made herself

ready...in fine linen, bright and clean; for the

fine linen is the righteous acts of the saints.

Revelation 19:7-8

16

🌿

A Pure and Holy Bride

As a pastor, one of the great pleasures of my ministry is sharing in the special moment when two become one in Christ as husband and wife. Wedding customs and traditions have changed over the years in many ways. Some couples still want the old traditional service complete with all the formal language as well as the "pomp and circumstance" and heraldry that goes hand in hand with that approach to conducting the wedding. Others opt for a more informal approach, writing their own vows, choosing music that is more contemporary than classical, and following forms that are more comfortable than ritualistic.

One of the more recent innovations in weddings since I started out as a pastor comes at the very end of the ceremony. After all the vows have been spoken and the rings, prayers, and pronouncements exchanged, most couples ask that I officially "present" them to the congregation as "Mr. and Mrs." That moment is a significant one for both, but especially for the bride who now has taken a new name and for the first time hears it in reference to herself. I love being able to make that official presentation of the couple and to watch with joy as the congregation often breaks out in spontaneous applause in response.

As we come to the end of this study about the Church, we have looked at what we are to do as a body of believers, how we are to do it, and why. But as we conclude, allow me to draw a picture of what should take place in the life of a church that actually puts these things into practice. We have stated that the Church's ultimate purpose is to glorify God, and we have taken a closer look at how we are to do that in two ways: what we do (the content of our ministry) and how we do it (the character of our ministry). However, we need to be reminded regularly of the big picture if we are to keep our focus clear in our minds. The end we have in mind is what Paul stated in Colossians 1:28: "...that we may **present** every man complete in Christ."

What an amazing moment that will be when we are presented as the Bride of Christ to the Bridegroom when He comes for us! Although a pastor may take great delight in presenting a bride and groom to the congregation at their wedding, it does not compare with the passionate delight we take in anticipating the day when the Church is presented as the Bride of Christ. Until then, we labor together in order that we may present every member complete in Christ so that He may be glorified in us as His holy Bride. What an honor it will be to be presented one day to the King of glory as the Bride He longs for! What a joy it will be to be present at the marriage supper of the Lamb of God, fully prepared with every detail finished, everything made perfect for that glorious day (Revelations 19:7-9)! But there still remains much to be done. What else do we need to get ready?

We Need Divine Intervention

> *"Christ also loved the church and gave Himself up for her...that He might present to Himself the church in all her glory, having no spot or wrinkle or any such thing; but that she should be holy and blameless." (Ephesians 5:25, 27)*

What an impossible task! How can you and I ever be completely pure, holy, and blameless? Only Christ Himself can make His own Bride ready for that day. Nothing we can do will ever prepare us sufficiently or in time. Restoring spiritual maturity must be a work of supernatural intervention in our lives, a spiritual intervention by which the grace of Christ accomplishes His work. Only by the power of the Lord at work within us, acting upon us and through us, will there ever be any hope of becoming perfect. Will we reach that state of perfection, that sinless condition, before we see Him face to face? No, because the work is still underway as the Holy Spirit continues to accomplish all that the Father desires to do in us.

But as the Church, His Bride, we have to yield to the hand of God preparing us for that day of presentation. In the wedding ceremony, the presentation of the bride and groom to the congregation marks a significant moment for the couple. But there is another moment that has even greater impact on the groom. After all the attendants have taken their places at the front, marching ceremoniously to their assigned spots, the suspense builds with the music as the bride steps into the doorway to enter the room. For that one breathtaking instant, there is nothing comparable to the magnificent splendor and beauty of that radiant woman as she stands there ready to become the wife of the awestruck groom.

Although traditions have changed and some no longer follow it, I love the custom of not allowing the groom to see his bride until she glides into view just before making her entrance. Even as a veteran of hundreds of weddings, I have to admit I still get a lump in my throat when the bride appears. Others all around me respond the same way as eyes moisten, knees weaken, and the toughest of fathers melts in the presence of the bride made ready for her husband.

That truly magical moment makes all the preparations worth it: the selection of the gown, the styling of the hair, and the hours of grooming and primping to get ready. We can only imagine how Jesus will feel when His Bride is finally ready to be presented to Him. By His own hand at work in our lives, He assures us that we will be made ready for that day as the Holy Spirit finishes the last touches necessary for us to be worthy of such a moment. Our readiness will be the result of His intervention on our behalf.

We Need a Perfect Model

How do we know what we are aiming for? When can we know that we are drawing closer to the goal of becoming His Bride? Hopefully the preceding chapters have offered you a better idea of how to answer those questions. But as long as we are living in this world, we need to understand that we still have a long way to go before we are made perfect. The reason for that is quite simple – we have not yet seen Christ as He is.

Even though we can learn much about Him and grow in our knowledge of Him through His Word and prayer, we still can only see Him through a glass dimly (1 Corinthians 13:12).

The apostle John wrote:

> *"Beloved, now we are children of God, and it has not appeared as yet what we shall be. We know that, when He appears, we shall be like Him, because we shall see Him just as He is. And everyone who has this hope fixed on Him purifies himself, just as He is pure." (1 John 3:2-3)*

Even though we will not be fully mature, perfect, or complete in every way until that day, we still are called to keep growing day by day toward Christlikeness.

Just as the bride prepares herself and plans months (sometimes years!) in advance for her wedding day, we must never think that we can postpone our preparation until the last day. Christ our Bridegroom goes before us and sets the standard of perfect holiness. He is beyond reproach, and He is already prepared – as He has been throughout all eternity!

By going before us, He raises our expectations of what we are to become, shows us what completeness really means, and reveals the essence of perfection in His glorious character. He is our perfect Model of what the finished work of our redemption will be when that final day comes, and His plan is accomplished in full in our lives as individuals and as the Church.

We Need Longterm Diligence

Completeness in Christ demands longterm diligence. Occasional nods to the ideals of the Christian faith can never be sufficient for the rigorous daily process of becoming what Christ calls us to be. We do positive harm within the body of Christ when we allow lukewarmness to creep into our lives. The Lord condemned that attitude in very harsh terms in His letter to the church in Laodicea, who allowed their love to cool even though they professed to be His disciples (Revelation 3:14-19).

I say "positive harm" because some people act as if there is nothing really wrong with confining our Christian experience to the routine and mundane activities of scheduled church activities. Leaving Christ out of every facet of life except a weekly visit to the church building is considered to be the normal Christian life by an alarming number who identify themselves as Christians.

Without realizing it, those who assume that they are well within their rights to do whatever they want actually retard the growth process of the Bride of Christ. No one would suggest that mature Christian people spring forth from the spiritual womb, but many live mindlessly as if there were nothing more to the Christian life than accepting Christ as Savior, joining a church, and then getting on with life.

God wants to break that pattern of thinking with this challenge for every believer. Following Christ demands the longterm diligence of keeping in step with the Spirit. Paul issued a similar exhortation to the Galatians: "If we live by the Spirit, let us also walk by the Spirit" (Galatians 5:25).[1] When God sets out to make us complete in Christ, He does not intend to hold back and settle for whatever we decide we can comfortably commit to Him. He calls us to be diligent, steadfast, faithful, and ready to pay any price so that we might be made complete in Him.

Two verses unlock this entire concept of "getting ready for the wedding" and have shaped much of my thinking about ministry over the past decade:

> *"And we proclaim Him, admonishing every man and teaching every man with all wisdom, that we may present every man complete in Christ. And for this purpose also I labor, striving*

---

1 The NIV translation says, "Since we live by the Spirit, let us keep in step with the Spirit" (Galatians 5:25).

according to His power, which mightily works within me."
(Colossians 1:28-29)

In this passage from Colossians, Paul uses two words to emphasize the diligence required to bring people to maturity in Christ. The first word is "admonishing," striking the note that we need strong admonition, exhortation, confrontation, and challenge in order to stick with our calling. Nowhere does he suggest that the process of maturing will be easy. In fact, the opposite is true – our growth is portrayed as costly and sometimes painful. Knowing our human nature, the Lord made it clear that we would need occasional words of warning, sometime stern warnings, if we are to stay on course. We must be reminded consistently of how far short we are of the goal of being made ready for the Bridegroom.

The second word Paul uses in these verses is "striving," or "agonizing," a term often used in the context of wrestling or in contests pitting strength against strength. We must realize that to be presented as complete in Christ we must endure times of intense labor. We must struggle to continue and fight the urge to give up and just sit out the rest of the race. Therefore, we all must strive together, agonizing over our condition as His Bride, longing for His coming for us. Are we where He wants us to be in the process of getting prepared, or are we ashamed of what He might still find when He arrives?

Once again, the illustration of a bride preparing for her wedding day reminds us of what needs to be done for us to be ready to be presented to Christ. If you have ever been around a bride and all those who are helping her get ready on the wedding day, you know what a hectic scene that can be. Nearly every wedding I have been a part of has been the same in this regard. Everyone is agonizing over last-minute details, checking and rechecking items that have been planned for months but are now supposed to be finished.

The adjustments to the gown are completed, the hair and make-up touched up one more time, the flowers and rings and gloves and veils and shoes and a host of other things I could never imagine are all reviewed one last time before the processional music begins. At long last the glorious moment of the presentation of the bride to the groom has arrived, and she takes the walk she has been waiting for all her life. She is now ready for her marriage to begin, knowing that the agonizing days of preparing and waiting are over.

Do you find it unusual that so few in the Church seem to be agonizing over our lack of readiness to meet the Bridegroom when He comes? One can hardly attribute our lack of concern to methodical and thorough preparedness. The truth is that we simply have not grasped what it means to Jesus to have His Church get ready. Or maybe we have cared too little.

A bridegroom would never forget the insensitivity and carelessness of an unkempt bride who did not bother to prepare for her wedding day. Why do we think that we can approach Christ as His Bride with so little interest in becoming all that He desires?

Hopefully this book has brought to your attention what He desires and helped you to see where you are and what remains to be done to get ready for His coming. Unlike the brides we know, the Bride of Christ does not know when the wedding day will be. Therefore, we have to be ready and pray, "Lord, make ready your Bride now! Prepare us and make us ready for that day. Perfect us so that we might be presented complete in Christ!"

How will your church be prepared? How will you be prepared? Will we be made ready – mature, complete, perfect as we grow up in Christ? Granted, when that day comes He will finish all that remains to be done. But what a wedding gift it would be to our Lord and Master if we were firmly rooted in the biblical principles and faithfully growing in the daily practices of what a church should be.

My prayer for the Church is that we will become so much like what He desires that others will be drawn to Him by the beauty they see in His Bride. I pray that He will instill in our hearts a longing to take what we have learned and trust Him enough to allow those things to be reproduced in us. To get there, we need to measure the effectiveness of each aspect of our ministry by its value in moving us further along toward completeness and maturity in Jesus Christ.

Will you commit yourself to a lifetime of being made ready by the Lord Jesus? Will you live for His return and joyfully anticipate that glorious moment when we are presented complete in Him to the Lamb of God Himself?

God has made the means available for all His purposes to be accomplished in the Church. He has opened His heart to us in His Word and shown us glimpses of the Bride He died for, longs for, and promises to return for. By the grace of Jesus Christ, we have been firmly rooted in Him and can continue to faithfully grow in Him right up to the day we are presented to Him:

> *"Let us rejoice and be glad and give glory to Him, for the marriage of the Lamb has come and His Bride has made herself ready....Blessed are those who are invited to the marriage supper of the Lamb." (Revelation 19:7, 9)*

Even so, come Lord Jesus! [2]

---

2 Revelation 22:20

Appendices

A MISGUIDED EMPHASIS
ON CHURCH GROWTH

CORE VALUES OF
PROVIDENCE BAPTIST CHURCH

ASKING THE RIGHT QUESTIONS

MOST FREQUENTLY ASKED QUESTIONS
ABOUT ELDER/DEACON STRUCTURE

A Misguided Emphasis on Church Growth

How did the Church ever get by for all these centuries without the benefit of the many books, tapes, and seminars now available that explain to leaders how they should run their ministries in the most efficient and effective way? With a quick glance at the current mass of resources pouring out of publishing houses and ministry centers, one would think that we have finally discovered what has until recently been hidden from pastors and Christian leaders. Condescending attitudes toward the ministries of previous generations that did not have the benefit of our modern methodology must surely be offensive to the One who has never failed to build His Church in His own way, whether in congregations of fifty or fifty thousand.

A new set of assumptions and expectations – radically different from the past – has sprung up about what it means to grow up a church in Christ. Like all assumptions, these must be carefully scrutinized to see if they have a biblical basis or a cultural one. We must be willing to ask whether our ideas about the body of Christ have been shaped by scriptural principles or by contemporary pragmatism. Just because we have happened upon an old truth once in a while and watched it burst the brittle and crusty wineskins of mindless church traditions, we cannot allow ourselves to believe that every new idea we have is going to revolutionize the Church in our time.

Some great ideas and challenging concepts have emerged from what has come to be called "the church growth movement." Churches are beginning to awaken from their dormancy and see that vibrant and exciting ministry does not have to be restricted to only New Testament times. The origins of this movement can be traced to those courageous few who dared to ask why most congregations in our Western culture seemed to follow the same methods, organize around the same structures, and experience the same lack of resemblance to what was described in Acts and the epistles.

Questions, penetrating and relentless questions, opened our eyes to reality. The Church was becoming more and more like the culture and having less and less to say to the culture. What could it say? It was as predictable and traditional as any other institution and quickly losing its ability to keep up with the rapid changes that were rocking the rest of society. New models for the Church were quickly met with enthusiastic approval among large segments of the nominally Christian world. Shrinking membership rolls began to bulge with curious seekers as creative leaders pioneered the uncharted territory of new ways of fulfilling our calling as the body of Christ.

The pioneers are still out there. New frontiers continue to give way as many are still asking questions, still looking for ways to allow the Holy Spirit to take us where we have never been before. Unfortunately, not as many are asking questions as there should be. Too many are blindly accepting the answers to someone else's questions and assuming that the answers to all church growth questions are of the one-size-fits-all category. Rather than pursuing our own answers, we have become just like those we loved to make fun of who were stuck in dull patterns of traditionalism, inherited largely from the eighteenth- and nineteenth-century models of small parish types of congregations.

If we are not careful, the same factors that led many generations of church leaders to accept uncritically and unquestioningly the way to "do church" will only lead us to become the new traditionalists. How ironic that one set of traditions has simply been exchanged for another by a new generation that prides itself on being different! Can the practices and methods of the church growth movement withstand careful scrutiny? Will the practitioners dare to ask questions, or will they dutifully fall in line and try to imitate what they perceive to be successful models of church growth?

Church growth can be a wonderful and glorious thing. My concern is that the recent gains in authentic church life will be reduced to nothing more than just another passing fad in the long history of the Church. We need to seriously examine what made the initial stages of the church growth movement so successful, both in spiritual and numerical growth. The answer is quite simple, and yet provides a framework within which many suspicious aspects of the church growth movement can be examined and their legitimacy called into question. How do we know when growth in a church is a good thing and when it is detrimental? The standard is simply this: *When God is the Author of growth, it will always be true to His nature and glorious to His name.*

The dangers in an unquestioning acceptance of a pragmatic, utilitarian church growth mentality should become apparent as we delve into what I call a misguided emphasis on church growth. Before launching into that list of dangers, let me first hasten to say that I am a firm believer in godly growth according to biblical principles.

A Healthy Church Is by Design a Growing Church

When a church follows God's plan, it will enjoy good spiritual health. The purposes and priorities of Jesus Christ for His Church have always produced vital congregations because He generates dynamic life in the hearts of His people.

The model in the book of Acts stands before us as a testimony of what can happen when a church fulfills its calling:

> *"Day by day continuing with one mind in the temple, and breaking bread from house to house, they were taking their meals together with gladness and sincerity of heart, praising God and having favor with all the people. And the Lord was adding to their number day by day those who were being saved." (Acts 2:46-47)*

Healthy churches do indeed give evidence of growth, sometimes spiritually, sometimes numerically. However, numerical growth does not always serve well in measuring church growth. Healthy churches *do* always grow, but this growth may not be seen in an increase in the number of people present.

Some of the most vibrant churches I know will probably never be considered growing churches because they are located in communities with a small and/or declining population. The prospect of ever reaching a thousand or even five hundred in attendance not only seems remote, but it would also require an airlift of people from surrounding cities to make it happen! However, the spiritual healthiness of these churches makes them growing churches because the members demonstrate a depth of understanding of the Lord and a quality of love and sacrificial service only possible by those who know Christ in a growing relationship.

Other growing churches might not be considered so because they have maximized their available space (using multiple services, auxiliary sites, and so on) and have no means to expand. Their vision emphasizes starting new congregations instead of allowing one to continue to increase in size beyond some arbitrary point upon which they have agreed. Transitioning and aging communities have made it necessary for some churches to redefine their ministry focus, but still remain true to their primary purpose of knowing Christ, making Him known, and growing to maturity in Him. There can be so many reasons growing churches do not experience numerical growth, not the least of which may be that the Lord has limited how far He will allow them to go.

If we are faithful to the calling of Christ and are growing mature men and women of God in our congregations, I am convinced that the Lord marks us as His growing churches. Why is that not enough anymore? Nearly every conference, every ministry brochure, every gathering of Christian leaders fosters the notion that the numbers must keep going up or else we have done something wrong. No longer does job satisfaction rest in seeing the miracle of men and women transformed by the power of the

Spirit. Taking the word of the leaders and participants in the church growth movement, the implication sometimes becomes the expectation – you must produce numbers if you are going to be a success in ministry.

As I have watched this phenomenon unfold over the past twenty-five years, I have developed a deep concern for the body of Christ and for those called to lead her. Unnecessary burdens and unrealistic expectations are ruining what would otherwise be happy, content congregations and leaders. Everyone seems to be afraid of failing. The pleasant thought of a pastor and a congregation growing in the grace and knowledge of Christ together through gentle years of faithful service has been all but eradicated as a legitimate model for ministry.

I began some time ago to list some of the concerns I have and have recently elevated them from concerns to danger signs. These represent what I believe to be a misguided emphasis on church growth, which will cost both the church and its leaders their very souls if not heeded. Each serves as a warning to me because I constantly have to keep them before me, lest I fall prey to their subtle and tempting promises of success. The relentless question before me continues to be, "Whose definition of success do I follow, God's or man's?"

A Growing Church Is Not Necessarily a Healthy Church

When we read the statistics, when we hear the boasts of the large numbers, let's face it. We are easily impressed. What I have come to realize is that size does not necessarily indicate the true spiritual vitality of a church. The potential dangers for the church growth movement can be found in the temptation to do whatever it takes to build the numbers and give every appearance of success. The cults stand as a ready witness. Unsound doctrine, actual heresy, has not diminished the ability of many cults and sects to attract followers, sometimes in massive numbers. Yet no one would argue for their spiritual health! We need wisdom to ask the right questions and then to avoid the dangerous pitfalls along the road to that elusive goal called a successful ministry.

1. *Selling out principles for the sake of attracting more people*

Principle-based ministry focuses the attention of both leaders and congregations on those things that really matter. If the principles most important to us as the Church are anchored in the Scriptures, then we can set our course by what we discover in God's Word. By their actions, churches have frequently confessed to giving higher value to principles derived more from Madison Avenue and popular marketing techniques than from the Bible.

When we embrace biblical principles, God's promises of blessing come with them. Without them, we are subject to every change in the direction of the wind. Blown about without proper foundations, advocates of church growth have lost sight of the primary reason the body of Christ exists. The Church was established to glorify God, to exalt the Lord Jesus Christ. In His Word, He has outlined in diverse fashion how we are expected to do just that. Once we have been distracted from that focus, we can be diverted to any course.

If the underlying goal and unstated purpose of the church growth movement is to fill up buildings with people, then biblical principles will prove to be problematic. There is an offense inherent in the gospel and a narrowness in the way of the cross that gravitate against the popularity of being a part of the body of Christ. The demands of discipleship cannot be diluted in an effort to make involvement in a local assembly of believers palatable to the masses.

Therein lies the dilemma. If we hold onto the principles revealed in the Scriptures, we run the risk of being unpopular with the crowds. Since we have seen that drawing big crowds has become the standard measurement for success, many churches and their leaders find themselves caught with conflicting values and priorities.

Any discussion beginning with the words, "We could get more people to come if..." is headed for trouble! All of us are guilty of sometimes trying to rationalize our decisions to compromise by couching our justifications in noble language. The truth is that we can easily compromise in subtle ways in order to attract more people and never be discovered.

We have to learn how to examine our hearts and discover our true motives. Genuine devotion to Christ and His Word will never sell short the cost of discipleship in an effort to gain a broader acceptance. We must watch for danger signs in what we do and how we do it so that we might detect and reject any drift toward the widespread practice of selling out our principles to attract more people.

2. *Focusing more on fruitfulness than on faithfulness*

God's calling to His disciples has never been focused on our ability to produce fruit. The contrary is actually true. If we assume the responsibility for what God alone can do, we will inevitably impair the nature of our relationship with Him and devote ourselves and our ministry leadership to that which cannot profit. Faithfulness is what the Lord expects from us. Fruitfulness is what He promises to bear through us. Performance-driven leaders and ministries struggle with this concept because it flies in the face of everything they hold dear and challenges their most fundamental source of satisfaction.

If we derive our satisfaction and contentment from our ability to get things done, to produce, we will always be suckers for every new gimmick that promises us greater success and productivity in our ministries. May the Lord help those poor souls who feel like failures in the sight of God and man if there is not significant progress and visible growth in their ministry life. They have bought the lie that they have worth only when there is something to show for their efforts, such as meeting quotas and reaching goals.

Such a focus on the results of our labors rather than the character of our labors always leads us farther from God, not closer. God calls us to be faithful and to leave the results, the bearing of fruit, in His hands. Any time I become more concerned about the fruitfulness of my ministry than the faithfulness of my ministry, I violate the very essence of what it actually means to serve Christ. I assume responsibility for what He alone can do and consequently deny Him by refusing to place my trust in Him and leave it there!

The Church cannot afford to follow leaders who usurp the role of the Holy Spirit and manufacture results on their own. Instead, the Church needs leaders who will fulfill their calling by simply doing their ministry in the power of the Holy Spirit and leaving the results to Him.

3. Becoming more anthropocentric than Christocentric (more reactive to the demands of man than proactive toward the priorities of Christ)

In a rather gradual way, the delicate balance of serving Christ and serving others has tilted in favor of developing ministry priorities based on human needs and demands rather than on divine mandate. Granted, we cannot ignore the vast range of human needs in setting the course of our ministry. Yet when that engine drives the train rather than sovereign design, we suffer for it.

Practically speaking, how much is our ministry vision determined by our desire to obey the Lord and fulfill His calling? How much of it is determined by regular evaluation and assessment of the human need around us, or the most demanding voices in our ears? The church growth movement has embraced an approach to ministry that is summed up in the words "seeker sensitive" and "need-based ministry." The idea behind these concepts is excellent. In our ministry, we should be aware of and sensitive to the needs of those we seek to reach. So far so good.

The problem unfolds when we adjust our ministry principles and priorities to attract people by promising to meet all the needs they think they have. Anthropocentric ministry derives its agenda from its focal point, "centered on man." Christocentric ministry derives its agenda from its focal point as well, but the central issue is Christ, not man.

Influenced by Urgencies or Priorities?

When the center of our attention is Jesus Christ, our priorities in ministry emerge from the context of our relationship with Him and our commitment to seek first His kingdom and righteousness. If we do not have a clear grasp of *our* biblical priorities and what issues are genuinely important in *our* lives, we can rest assured that someone else will be quick to provide us with *theirs*.

When church growth becomes more important to us than discovering God's will for our lives, we will jump at every demand placed before us that promises to be the "secret" that will throw us into the land of the "megachurch." Nearly every pastor I know could write a book listing all the diverse secrets shared by zealous friends of the ministry. If we answered the urgent calls to chase first this plan or that priority, we would run from pillar to post for the rest of our days, never resting and never finding any peace. The frustration of living reactively in response to urgent demands rather than moving proactively toward our priorities has exhausted many earnest servants who confused zealous busyness with knowledgeable and wise action.

The only preventive measure against this kind of misguided emphasis on hectic activity is to establish clearly defined biblically-based priorities and then build a proactive ministry that keeps those priorities and principles ever before you.

By God's design, when we fulfill our calling to keep Christ at the center of all that we do, we will prosper in our ministry in such a way that the needs of those around us will be met. However, if we allow our agenda to be determined by needs, we may or may not meet those human needs, and we will certainly not succeed in glorifying Christ and advancing His kingdom. If we aim at the former, we will hit both the former and the latter. If we aim at the latter, in all likelihood we will miss the latter and without question miss the former.

Our ministries must remain Christocentric in every way, not anthropocentric. Churches that lose sight of this fundamental principle may appeal to many who like to be the center of attention, but in the long run there probably will be no long run. Without roots in the unshakable foundation of Christ, ministries that are man-centered may create quite a stir in the first gusts of activities, but soon are gone with nothing to show for their efforts but good intentions:

> *"Now if any man builds on the foundation with gold, silver, precious stones, wood, hay, straw, each man's work will become evident; for the day will show it because it is to be revealed with fire, and the fire itself will test the quality of each man's work."* (1 Corinthians 3:12-13)

Any focus other than Christ will be revealed one day. Christian ministry must constantly check its bearings to be sure that Christ is indeed the center from which everything else proceeds. Only what is done in Him will last.

4. *Emphasizing a ministry team that is more professional than pastoral*

Shifts in the culture generally affect the Church as well. We should impact the culture more than be impacted by it, but the fact remains that we in the body of Christ often reflect the changes undergone in society whether positively or negatively. Academics have long been lauded as an elite group in the informal social stratification of our nation. Recently however, an even higher value seems to have been given to the accumulation of degrees and titles, especially among those who are traditionally viewed as professionals. Master's and doctoral degrees that once were expected only in certain fields have become *de rigueur* as the number of positions now considered professions instead of occupations have increased.

Among those positions elevated to professional status is that of pastor, or any other church ministry position requiring advanced study and training. The concern I have arises not so much from the perspective that ministry positions are considered professions, but that pastors and church leaders have allowed such terminology to shift their approach from one of a pastoral calling to that of a professional position.

A Misguided Emphasis on Church Growth

In his book, *No Place for Truth,* David Wells addresses this concern:

> "The Christian ministry has become a profession. In today's seminaries, Edward Farley observed, the 'theological student neither studies divinity nor obtains scholarly expertise in theological sciences, but trains for professional activities.'...The yearning for wisdom is thus transformed into a yearning to look more like a skilled lawyer, psychologist, or business executive than an ordained minister of the gospel, marching to the beat of the transcendent Drummer."[1]

Just this week, I talked with a reporter from a local newspaper who asked if I had given much thought to pursuing a master's degree in business administration since so much of what a pastor does these days requires that expertise. For the reporter, the question was natural. Why not get the academic credentials of a "professional" since the expectations of the position suggest that course of action?

Among pastors, the sense that their calling has lost some of its prestige has led many to spend a disproportional amount of time and energy reinforcing their value, both in their own eyes as well as the community they serve. The identification of themselves as servant-leaders, simple shepherds, bold prophets, faithful teachers, and compassionate counselors plays a very small role in their aspirations. After all, if the criteria set forth by search committees tell us anything, the biblical qualifications for someone called to function in Christian ministry take a distant backseat to other more pressing issues. Churches do not seem to be looking for someone with a heart for God as much as they are someone with a head for figures. They mention that they would prefer a pastor who is a good preacher (however that is to be defined), but it is an absolute requirement that he be strong in administration and counseling.

---

1 David Wells, *No Place for Truth* (Grand Rapids: William B. Eerdmans Publishing Company, 1993), 112-14.

In all honesty, churches that reflect these shifts in our cultural thinking have the ability to get things done. When the emphasis changes from the priority of ministry to the priority of management, the results may be profound in efficiency and organizational stability. However, if we are not careful, we may foster a climate that produces professional technicians who know how to "do church" but have lost the soul of their ministry in the process.

The temptation to move in this direction is so subtle. As our own congregation has grown, the need for better organization and communication has increased proportionately. We have made great progress in learning how to do things "decently and in order" so that there is integrity in what we do and how we do it. We have our organizational charts, our policies, and our planning processes and hope to accomplish what we are called to do more effectively and efficiently. But in many occasions, normal business procedures and the standards by which decisions are made have to be set aside in order to follow the leadership of the Holy Spirit. When we refuse to take steps of faith because such actions would violate logical business principles, we may maintain fiscal stability and sound organizational structure but miss the blessing of the Lord!

Driven by the Bottom Line or Called to Eternal Purposes?

I must always be aware of the tendency I have seen in myself and others to be *driven* by the bottom line of professionalism rather than *called* to the eternal purposes of pastoral ministry. The questions being asked among those on the bandwagon of church growth have more to do with whether it works, rather than whether it is biblical. In terms of the bottom line, many activities and programs are evaluated on the query, "If we build it, will they come?"

If we chose to chart a radical course of biblical obedience and no one was interested, would our ministry be considered a success or a failure? We will in all likelihood never know because the Lord always seems to have seven thousand who have not bowed the knee to Baal (1 Kings 19).

But if it was possible, we could be wonderfully blessed with monumental growth spiritually and never see any numerical counterpart. However, this does not seem to be an acceptable possibility for proponents of church growth.

The bottom line can effectively come to matter more than our eternal calling if we do not watch carefully and guard our hearts. As our ministry has made necessary changes in the way we function, I found out something about myself in the process. I actually like to have people tell me how "professionally" we do our job. A high form of flattery to me, I have discovered, is to tell me and others on our staff that we are doing things that would be a credit to any organization, secular or sacred. Is there anything wrong with doing things right? Not at all! But enjoying and being impressed by the idea that people note a professional nature in me should not appeal to me more than the favor of the One who actually called me. When this happens, it should send up blazing flares warning me that my heart has shifted with the culture. May the Lord protect me and my fellow servants in ministry from the siren call to become more professional at the expense of being more pastoral!

5. *Striving to become smarter and better informed instead of more godly and Christlike*

The aforementioned emphasis on academics and the accompanying education fixation in our culture have produced a mentality in the body of Christ that places an extremely high value on amassing information. If knowing how to operate one computer program is good, then knowing how to operate multiple programs is great!

This mentality has invaded the Church and presented us with a generation of believers who value information for the sake of information, not because of the benefit that information could bring if applied in practical daily living. Now more than ever, Christians do not want to admit ignorance on any subject. As a result, there are many church members who place a premium on their ability to cite chapter and verse on any imaginable subject, but who are unwilling to apply the Word in their daily walk with Christ.

Busy Lives Versus Purposeful Lives

Churches view themselves as successful if they can point to the breadth of their teaching and discipling curriculum, the high level of involvement of people in weekly (or several times a week is even better) studies, and the biblical literacy rate among their members. Often among churches in my own denomination, the most telling statistic regarding stable church growth is the percentage of people who are regularly engaged in some meaningful study of biblical topics and books.

How involved do you think someone needs to be before we can say that we have assimilated them into the life of the ministry? Busy people can serve as an indication of a healthy, spiritually mature congregation, or they can be nothing more than window dressing – there for show but not substantive and real beyond the surface appearance.

Since the church growth movement emphasizes evaluating the level of involvement of ministry participants, the busier we can keep our people the better off we are. I am neither convinced that this is profitable nor am I impressed that this is a sign of a healthy congregation. An active, aggressive, ministering people will indeed find their place in ministry, but they will do so in a balanced approach to their walk with Christ.

When we begin to expect everyone to participate in everything we make available, we seriously cut into our credibility that we desire them to maintain strong relationships with Christ, their families, coworkers, and others in their lives. Is an event successful if only a few people support it, if only a few already busy people participate in it? The answer must be crafted from a sane estimation of the purpose of the event or ministry. We cannot reasonably expect God's blessings on our guilt-enforced, coerced attempts to keep people so busy that they have no time to find and fulfill His purposes in their lives.

God's standard has more to do with whether we are "doers, not hearers only" (James 1:22). Amassing volumes of information without an accompanying commitment to application leads to spiritual dryness, even if it arises in the midst of doctrinally sound thinking. Are we more concerned about information than about transformation, about the mind than the heart? While avoiding the trap of over-involvement and mindless busyness, we still have a responsibility to mature in all aspects of our faith, demonstrating maturity and wisdom both in what we know and what we do.

6. Preferring more to be entertained by the quality of our productions than awed by the majesty of God

"Bigger and better, new and improved" – familiar words to us, but are they representative of what honors the Lord in ministry? If we are not careful, we can buy into that way of thinking. Each Sunday morning worship service succeeds only as it surpasses the previous week's efforts in the quality of the music, the eloquence and depth of the sermon, the flow of its component parts (as if the service was a well-oiled machine), and the overall impact made on the "audience." In other words, was the "production" a success in terms of its interest and entertainment value?

The only legitimate audience in a church is the audience of One to whom all of our attention must be given. He is the One by whom all of our endeavors are to measured against the holy standard of His righteous Son. Even the idea of coming together for the purpose of "getting something out of" the planned event goes against the grain of what it means to enter the Lord's presence with awe before His majesty and splendor.

Quality in what we do can be motivated by a desire to give Christ our best, but it can also be an excuse to boost our own egos as we build figurative towers of Babel simply to prove what we can do. Therefore, we must establish some limits lest our tendency toward one-up-manship takes over and rules our thinking. For example, we laid out some guidelines early on when we began to offer Christmas and Easter musicals as evangelistic efforts so that we would not be tempted to outdo the previous year's offering. Such self-limiting is necessary to curb our natural drift toward entertaining bigger and better, rather than directing our focus to the awe inspired by the majesty of God.

7.   *Tending to be more impressed by numbers than impacted by holiness*

When someone asks you how things went in your church this past Sunday, what criteria do you use to answer such a question? How we make that assessment goes a long way toward revealing what impresses us.

If you ask many pastors on Monday how things went over the weekend, I am embarrassed to say that the answer will most likely have to do with how many people attended their Sunday meetings. If attendance was high, in all likelihood, the answer will be that it was a glorious day, full of joy. If attendance dropped, no matter what else happened, the day is evaluated in the shadow of that cloud.

On many occasions, I have had gracious friends speak to me after a worship service in which the Lord had spoken powerfully through His Word and His Spirit had moved in a significant way. However, with the best of intentions, they attempted to console me about the lack of any visible response at the time of public invitation given at the end of the service. The standard by which we tend to be impressed is in the numbers who respond, who attend, who give, but seldom do we employ the standard of that subjective presence or absence of an awareness of the holiness of God revealed as we worshiped Him.

8.   *Responding more to an appeasement of the convenient than to an appeal to sacrifice*

Wouldn't it be wonderful if everyone was perfect? Motivated by noble purposes and guided by selfless ends, we would all function wholeheartedly for the glory of the Lord and for the benefit of all. Instead, we face the ever-present reality that most people do not get involved in anything without some sense of personal gain firmly settled in their minds. The "me generation" of baby boomers has succeeded in convincing many churches that the only way to get them to come and participate is to meet their terms.

Entirely too much attention has been given to making discipleship convenient and service for Christ adjustable to one's chosen lifestyle. How must all of this sound to a Savior who bids us come and die with Him and if necessary for Him? We are trying to do what Jesus said was impossible. We are working diligently to make following Christ easy, to make our manner of ministry comfortable, and to make personal sacrifice obsolete.

You get what you pay for. If we bring people into our ministries believing that we are there for them instead of them being there for Christ, we deserve the inevitable whining and complaining that will surely follow!

9. Desiring popularity and a good reputation rather than piety and a sound character

Like it or not, what people think of us usually does matter to us. Everyone likes to be liked. When people think about our church, I want them to think favorably about us. The way I respond when I discover that there is someone who disagrees with me or does not have a high regard for our church lets me know that something in me still longs to maintain everyone's favor.

Am I concerned more about popularity than piety? I would like to think not, but I must admit that being popular and having a good reputation appeals to me more than being regarded with disdain and having people always think ill of me. However, I cannot afford to allow such sentiments to shape the character of my ministry. After all, reputation is nothing more than what we appear to be to others, whereas our character is what we are in fact to the Lord. Since He is more concerned with our piety than with our popularity, I should be also.

But a misguided emphasis on church growth may lead us to do things to retain our popularity at the expense of faithfulness to Christ. If we resist taking stands on unpopular issues (abortion, homosexuality, racial prejudices, or even the gospel itself) in order to win the favor of the general population, we will forsake our integrity and faithfulness to Christ. Many mistakenly believe they will win more souls for Christ if they do not take unpopular stands. Instead, their wishy-washy posture serves to erode any credibility they may have had about the value of their faith (if it has value, why so quickly compromise it?).

10. Pursuing excellence more for the sake of pride than for the glory of Christ

A commendable feature of the church growth movement has been its insistence that Christ and the work that represents Him through the Church should be of the highest possible quality. We should indeed insist on excellence for Christ.

Like any other noteworthy matter, this one can be easily perverted and twisted in a worthless direction. If we do not exercise the greatest caution, our own desires and pride can dominate our activities and overtake our proclamations that we do what we do only because we want the best for Christ. The truth is that we want the best, but if we strip away all of the pretense, we want it to be the best so that we can take pride in what we have done, not so that Christ gets the very best. We in fact keep the very best, the glory and the credit, for ourselves.

Only the Lord can know our motives perfectly. We can even fool ourselves with all of our rhetoric. Excellence for Christ will always be consistent with His character. The only effective measure for our own motivation is to look not only to the end we are striving to achieve, but to the means by which we are laboring. Both ends and means must match the character of Christ before any glory will be lifted up to Him.

By taking the time to list all of these potential pitfalls, there is a risk of being accused of making excuses for not growing. One can easily see how a ministry could take advantage of these warnings to rationalize its failure to follow Christ into fields of healthy spiritual growth. In the event that someone might misunderstand my intent, I repeat what I said as I introduced this subject: a healthy church is indeed a growing church. I pray that every ministry God ever allows me to be a part of will be considered a growing ministry from His perspective.

However, when any of these aforementioned symptoms arise, we can be sure that the spiritual health and growth of the body of Christ is at stake. There may be quantifiable numerical growth, but it will have no roots and will soon wither and blow away as dust in the wind. Borrowing from the words of 2 Kings 19:30, we must continue to commit ourselves to "**take root downward** and bear **fruit upward**." God's plan for church growth makes it absolutely essential to be "**firmly rooted** and now being **built up in Him and established**" in our faith (Colossians 2:7). Only that which the Lord builds up brings glory to His name. Everything else always proves to be worthless effort.

Our calling is to take care of the *depth* of the ministry by following Jesus Christ wherever He leads and to leave the *breadth* of our ministry to Him!

Core Values of
Providence Baptist Church

What makes one church different from another? If we look at the principles upon which their ministries are established or even their basic goals and purposes, we will not find too much to distinguish one evangelical church from another. Yet when we visit different churches we are struck by how unique each one really is.

Each church develops its own personality and style of ministry according to the special mix of individual members the Lord assembles together in that one place. Just as different recipes produce different flavors, the Lord blends His people in churches to achieve the distinctive taste that suits Him the most, capitalizing on the great variety present in those who have gathered to serve Him in each congregation.

Some of the distinctiveness arises from the cultural setting of the Church, some from the socioeconomic mix, some from the spiritual gifts of the members, and some from the ministry style and preferences of the leadership. Yet as much as each of these contributes to a church's uniqueness, there is still a larger contributing factor than any of these – the core values of the congregation. Within a biblical framework, each body of believers develops its own closely held values and seeks to promote those values in carrying out its ministries.

At Providence, we have tried to define what those values are so that all who come to participate in the ministry here will know what to expect in our life together. Problems arise in congregations where there are differing assumptions about what the priorities should be and what should be valued most highly. Therefore, we want to make sure that new members understand our core values so that there are no surprises about what makes our ministry distinctive from other churches. Just as a clear statement of purpose unites us, so will a summary of our ministry distinctives and core values.

Misunderstanding and miscommunication are often the result of differing assumptions. As a young pastor eager to start a new church, I worked hard to define in my own mind what kind of church I believed it should be. Much of that definition took shape as I searched for biblical principles upon which a ministry should be built. I tried to rule out various models inconsistent with what I believed the Lord wanted to accomplish in our fledgling congregation.

With that vision in mind, I spoke often to visitors and prospective members about the direction we felt the Lord leading. Invariably people were gracious and shared my excitement. Once in a while though, a few would express reservations about aspects of the vision. When that happened, I would back off in order not to run them away. Unfortunately, on more than one occasion, I realized I was compromising on an issue, so I could impress those I was talking to and encourage them to join our congregation.

Years later an honest friend pointed out something that troubled me greatly because it was true. He told me that the most significant struggles and disagreements our church had suffered had been on the points of the vision on which I had compromised. As it turned out, the people I had sought to appease and impress were not satisfied with the concessions I had already made, but actually became more demanding as time went by, insisting that the very nature of the ministry change to suit their personal tastes and preferences.

The interesting twist, though, was this: in nearly every case I was left "holding the bag," as the expression goes. The people for whom I sold out my principles to please eventually left the church to try to find *another* church that was more like the one they wanted. Once they were gone, I found that trying to restore compromised principles was far more difficult than staying on course from the beginning. The temptation of trying to attract people who do not share the same vision for ministry only serves to frustrate everybody.

As a result of this experience, I again turned to the Scriptures and asked myself, "What does God value most for our church?" After much prayer and study, I developed a list of twelve biblically-based values (or ministry distinctives). Our congregation embraced these values, known today as our church's core values. We believe in these values with all our hearts and vow never to compromise them again, by the grace of God.

If you could describe what makes your calling and ministry distinct from others, what would you list? Each congregation has its own core values, whether they are actually identified or not, and they play a significant role in determining where members choose to focus their energies. Taking the time to ascertain your core values will help clarify direction and establish a basis for assessing the relative value of the numerous alternatives we face in approaching ministry.

Although most evangelical churches will affirm these same values to one degree or another, we consider these twelve most important and do our best to maintain them in a proper balance as the ministry grows toward maturity in Jesus Christ. These twelve core values provide a framework for understanding who we are and why we do what we do as the body of Christ here at Providence Baptist Church.

1.   THE CENTRALITY OF JESUS CHRIST

In every aspect of our ministry, the focal point must always be the honor and glory of the Lord Jesus Christ, the living Head of the body who is now exalted gloriously at the right hand of the Father. If we deviate from this pivotal focus, nothing else will help correct our course. Until the purpose of every area of ministry, the goal of every activity, is to seek His praise and glory, we will find that our ministry is in vain.

Paul reminds us to "keep seeking the things above, where Christ is, seated at the right hand of God" (Colossians 3:1) and to "press on toward the goal for the prize of the upward call of God in Christ Jesus" (Philippians 3:14). We are also told to fix "our eyes on Jesus, the author and perfecter of faith, who for the joy set before Him endured the cross, despising the shame, and has sat down at the right hand of the throne of God" (Hebrews 12:2). In everything, we are to make sure that our focus is on Christ.

Therefore, as simple as it sounds, we want to emphasize and re-emphasize the surpassing value of knowing Christ and pursuing our ministry in such a way that He is central, preeminent in all things. The first level through which every question of our ministry must pass is whether or not it affirms the centrality of Jesus Christ.

2. THE INERRANCY OF THE BIBLE

The authority for our ministry comes from the Word of God as we submit ourselves to its teaching, commit ourselves to do what it says, and yield our lives to become what Christ desires for us to be. We believe that its truth and its authority call forth from us a response of obedience and submission.

What we know about Jesus Christ, what we have discovered about the Father and the Holy Spirit, what we have learned about the nature of the human race, all have been revealed in God's Word. Providence will always devote a significant proportion of time and energy to teaching and proclaiming the Bible and holding it forth as the standard of truth and righteousness.

As we apply the Scriptures to the practical aspects of life, our lives will change daily by the power of the Holy Spirit who wants to conform us to the image of Christ. The second level through which every issue of our ministry must pass then is whether or not it lines up with the Word of God, either in principle or precept.

3. THE UNDERGIRDING OF PRAYER

One of the greatest influences on my understanding of prayer outside the Scriptures has been the writings of E. M. Bounds,[1] an American pastor

---

1 E. M. Bounds, *The Complete Works of E.M. Bounds on Prayer* (Grand Rapids, Michigan: Baker Book House, 1990) 76.

in the late nineteenth and early twentieth centuries. Here are his thoughts on the importance of prayer to the spiritual vitality of the body of Christ:

> "As God's house is, preeminently, a house of prayer, prayer should enter into and underlie everything that is undertaken there. Prayer belongs to every sort of work pertaining to the church of God. As God's house is a house where the business of praying is carried on, so is it a place where the business of making praying people out of prayerless people is done. The house of God is a divine workshop, and where the work of prayer goes on....Any church calling itself the house of God, and failing to magnify prayer; which does not put prayer in the forefront of its activities; which does not teach the great lesson of prayer, should change its teaching to conform to the divine pattern or change the name of its building to something other than a house of prayer."

All that we do must have the thorough undergirding of individual and corporate prayer or else there can be no reason to anticipate the attending power and presence of the Holy Spirit in our ministry. Without a foundation of prayer, the activity of a group of believers is stripped of any eternal effectiveness. The church that does not bathe its ministry in fervent prayer, or invest its best energies in faithful prayer, or make prayer its first order of business will never enjoy the fruitful ministry the Lord has prepared for it. When prayer slips from the priority position it must have, the Church may engage in whatever endeavor it pleases, but will never accomplish the purposes of God until the rank and file of the congregation together commits to the rigorous labors of praying.

A major difference exists between a church that *believes* in prayer, and the church that actually *prays*. We can believe in it without doing it, but the ministry is not undergirded properly until we set ourselves to praying. Only then will the work of Christ be built upon a foundation of consistent communion and communication with the Lord. Therefore, we must frequently ask ourselves: Have we given ourselves sufficient time to pray? What grievous errors in the life of any congregation could have been avoided had time been taken to seek the Father's heart and mind in prayer?

4.   AN ENVIRONMENT OF GRACE

Convinced of the absolute sovereignty of a holy God, we understand that nothing good happens in our ministry that is not the result of His grace, His unmerited favor toward us. Consequently, our ministry together must be characterized by that same grace in our response to one another.

In a very practical way, every relationship in the Church should provide models of grace in action. The way we treat one another will always be the truest test of our credibility in what we say we believe. If our relationships are marked by pettiness, selfishness, rudeness, grudges, suspicion, and all sorts of other signs of distrust and lack of love, we may be sure that we are not enjoying an environment where grace prevails. However, if we treat one another with respect, unconditional love, an attitude of servanthood, a readiness to forgive and look for the best in each other, we will witness a revolutionary transformation of the lives around us. We will see what happens when failing does not mean condemnation, when mistakes are met with a perspective that gives people the benefit of the doubt.

Few things make life more pleasant than knowing that there is freedom to fail. Far from creating a sloppy tolerance for inferior efforts, that freedom to fail makes it possible for people to be bold in trying new things, venturing forth into the unknown more confidently, walking by faith more securely. An environment of grace brings freedom because we know that we can expect a loving response from others around us in the ministry whether we earned it or not. Grace from the Lord enables us to give grace to others, without condemnation, without looking out for ourselves, but responding to others in the way we would want them to respond to us.

Therefore, every person we meet in our day-to-day walk with Christ must be able to recognize His grace at work in us. The fourth level of scrutiny then is to measure our ministries to see if there is indeed an environment of grace being presented and perpetuated by the attitude and demeanor of the body of Christ.

5. A DECENTRALIZED MINISTRY

Decentralizing our ministry means that our highest goal will *not* be getting everyone to come to the church (the physical building) to meet. Ministry must take place out in the midst of a fallen world. When we do meet together, we want to equip our members to effectively minister to the thousands of everyday people who will never darken the door of a church building, but who nonetheless need Christ. Our challenge is to provide balance by not asking members to gather together so often that they have no time to actually minister.

The tendency is to try to bring the ministry back to the equipping center, rather than pressing forward into unknown regions where human need makes itself known, unmasked and without pretense. It feels safer to believers to gather with their own kind, to compare notes about how we are faring in the hostile environment outside the church, and maybe to feel a little superior to folks who have not yet discovered the answers we already have. But when the body of Christ turns itself inward, it loses its sense of mission and its evangelistic purpose.

Centralizing the ministry is convenient, simpler, and certainly more safe and secure. The problem is that it fosters the wrong notion. It somehow gives the impression that the Church is a place separate from the rest of the world where we can escape. Yet God's Word indicates that the Church has been sent out, commissioned, and charged with duties to serve notice to the world that Jesus Christ is still Lord of all. Therefore, this fifth value of decentralized ministry serves as a check to keep us from slipping quietly into oblivion and leaving our world without a viable word of hope from the people of God.

6.   A MISSIONS AND EVANGELISM EMPHASIS

Evangelism can never be viewed as either an alternative ministry, or a ministry that churches do as a special project once in a while. It must be a part of the fabric of our lives.

Love compels us to go and tell others about Christ. Because we love Him, we cannot stop talking about Him and what He has done in our lives. Because He has loved us, we can genuinely love others in His name and want them to know Him too. The location for evangelism and missions does not matter. A heart for Christ and for the people He came to save makes all the difference as to whether or not we commit ourselves to leading others to know Him.

The value of a human soul compelled Christ to lay aside His privilege and to take the form of a bondservant – even to the point of death on the cross (Philippians 2:7-8). Can we ever afford to devalue what God prized so highly? In the eyes of the Father, the worth of one soul was such that He willingly gave His only Son to die for that soul. Therefore, we must continue to emphasize evangelism and missions, both at home and far away, wherever there are those who have not been given the privilege of hearing of the matchless grace of Jesus Christ.

What will distinguish us as a unique people after God's own heart? We must have this sixth core value fixed in our hearts and minds as we plan for ministry. Whether we are praying for a neighbor to come to know the Lord, or preparing to go overseas as career missionaries, each of us has a role to play in God's plan for introducing the people of His world to Jesus Christ.

7.   ACCOUNTABILITY OF SMALL GROUPS

The people who tend to drift away from the body of Christ are most often those who never plugged in, who never allowed anyone close enough to know them and express love for them. The same is true of those who fall into sin, whose zeal for the things of God cools as the ember gets separated from the bed of coals. Integrity in the lives and ministries of our members requires that the Church provide a context for accountability relationships by giving priority to the development of small groups.

As congregations grow numerically, it is quite easy for an individual to gravitate toward the posture of a spectator. Hiding among the crowd allows a person to become almost anonymous. Without meaningful relationships with others within the context of smaller, more personal fellowship groups, a church member can avoid any accountability for his or her walk with Christ.

A conscientious effort must be made to enfold each person into a small group of believers who know and care about what is happening in that person's life. If this effort is not made, the larger congregation will become a dysfunctional family of individuals who have no connection to one another. Loneliness is a terrible condition, but it is even worse when it is experienced in the midst of a crowd. We have a responsibility to reach out and to help people find their place, assist them in meeting others who care about them, and follow through with them until they have found their place alongside friends who will engage them in meaningful relationships.

Whenever I have noticed that people have slipped into a state of carelessness, or into a pattern of sporadic involvement, or even into a period of neglect of their spiritual lives, whatever the initial impetus, the factor that contributes most to their inactivity is the absence of fellowship with others in a small group of Christian friends. Therefore, we have come to place a high value on the importance of encouraging everyone to find a place in a small group in order to find practical expressions of the love that the Lord wants us to share together.

Sadly, many refuse to allow themselves to experience the benefits of small groups, or they do not recognize how significant it is to their spiritual health. Once a congregation gets beyond the first fifty to a hundred members, it cannot thrive without smaller groups who support and encourage each other. Those who look to the pastors, the elders, the deacons, or to other church leaders to give them their significance will find themselves quickly disappointed. However, if they will allow themselves to become a part of a small group, they will find great contentment in engaging others in the sweet communion of the Spirit.[2] The accountability of small groups, this seventh ministry distinctive, must be maintained if the Church is to be healthy in its growth in Christ.

8. THE IMPORTANCE OF THE FAMILY

Solid, biblical family relationships are essential to the family unit's ability to function as God intended, and godliness in the family is a priority for the body of Christ. Even in the biblical qualifications for elders and deacons, a man's family is considered a valuable standard for measuring his maturity in Christ. Many churches have so emphasized commitment to the ministry of the local church that they have missed the obvious biblical priority of the family. How many thousands of homes have been sacrificed on the altar of a successful church ministry? Yet God calls us to serve Him at home before we are qualified to serve Him elsewhere. Leaders in the church need to commit themselves to spending time with their families, bringing them along to share in the life of the church, and teaching them to know and love the Lord God.

Within our culture, few models exist of proper relationships in families, even though families form the very building blocks of society. It is the Church's responsibility to provide models and to offer training from God's Word about how parents and children are to relate to one another and about the biblical principles of marriage. Terms like sacrifice and submission, which have fallen upon deaf ears in our selfish culture, must be rediscovered by those who would be disciples of Jesus Christ in their marriages, just as much as in the rest of their daily walk with Him. Effective churches are committed to strengthening families by the faithful application of God's principles, both by precept and by example, so that we may grow up families the way God designed them.

---

2 I have often marveled at the people who get together for fellowship with one another in order to complain about the lack of fellowship in their church! They are so close to finding what they are looking for among others of a kindred spirit that they cannot see what they already have found. If they would shift the purpose of their relationship from a negative, complaining one to a positive, encouraging one, they would realize the joy involved in sharing life together in Christ.

Recognizing that one of the greatest battlefields and proving grounds of our faith is right within the home, we are committed to strengthening the spiritual lives of families as they seek to become beacons of light for Christ within our community. As we proceed in the development of a balanced approach to life and ministry as a congregation, we must keep in mind how our plans, schedules, and activities contribute to the growth of strong, loving families among our members.

This eighth value is a significant factor in how we think about what we do, how often we are away from our families to engage in ministry, and how we can make a greater impact on our homes throughout every level of our ministry.

9.   THE SIGNIFICANCE OF HUMBLE SERVANTHOOD

Our ministry is built upon the assumption that there is no task, no responsibility, beneath any of our members so that we undertake every ministry with a humble heart, grateful for the privilege of serving Christ and His body. With so much attention in our culture given to status and position, to power and prestige, when every member in the body of Christ demonstrates servanthood in action, people notice that something is different.

Ministry is a privilege, a holy calling. Yet it is not a calling where special privileges or special treatment should be expected. Unfortunately, those who would rather be served far outnumber those who are willing to serve. That tragic reality need not remain true for those who have committed themselves to follow Jesus Christ. In fact, it cannot remain true if we do follow Him, for He said,

> *"You know that the rulers of the Gentiles lord it over them, and their great men exercise authority over them. It is not so among you, but whoever wishes to become great among you shall be your servant, and whoever wishes to be first among you shall be your slave; just as the Son of Man did not come to be served, but to serve, and to give His life a ransom for many." (Matthew 20:25-28)*

If servanthood is the calling of the Master, it is right to expect it to be the calling of those who would follow Him. There is something singularly winsome about one who has a servant's heart. All the more is that true when that value is demonstrated throughout the body of Christ.

When we demonstrate a willingness to serve one another in the name of Jesus Christ, the credibility of our testimony to the life-changing power of our Savior gains significantly. Conversely, if we ever turn down a duty, if we ever neglect some task, thinking that someone "less than I" will see to it, the seeds of our ruin will have been sown. Hence, we see the high value placed in the Scriptures on humble servanthood and the reason we have so emphasized it here in our ministry together. This ninth level of emphasis allows us to ask ourselves as we face any new challenge, any new task, "Will I choose to serve, or be served, in the direction I go and in the ministry I pursue?"

10. AN EMPHASIS ON FAITHFULNESS, NOT FRUITFULNESS

So much of the measure of a church in recent days has been focused on the outward evidences of its apparent success. The number of people present, the amount of money given, the size of the facilities, the breadth of its programming, and so on have been used as the criteria by which a church succeeds or fails. All of these things can present an impression of great effectiveness when in reality, in the eyes of the Lord, there is no fruit being born at all for His name.

When a congregation begins to aim for becoming bigger and better rather than for becoming more faithful in obeying the voice of the Master, it loses sight of its reason for existence. Being faithful as a goal will sometimes produce more fruitful congregations. But trying to become ever more fruitful can get in the way of being faithful. Looking to improve the "vital statistics" of the ministry is fine, if they are defined as the evidence of the character of Christ in the lives of the people. But more than likely, these statistics are defined as numbers present, dollars given, and facilities constructed (the emphasis on "bodies, budgets, and buildings"). When that is the case, being faithful will hinder progress and growth and is often the victim of compromises made to keep things moving forward.

Although the ministry of Providence may never "produce" large numbers, we will still be successful in God's eyes if we remain true to our calling, faithful to Him above all else. The value placed on faithfulness is clear in God's Word. Growth for the sake of growth will not bring honor to the Lord – but faithful obedience does.

11. A STREAMLINED/TARGETED MINISTRY

Human nature being what it is, whatever ministry we are involved in usually seems to us to be the most important one on earth. We often think, "If God called me to such an important ministry, He must have called everyone else in the church to the same one." However, God calls us to different ministries according to our gifts, our temperaments, the special things for which our life experiences have prepared us, and other reasons known only to Himself. As a result, we should not expect that He will call everyone to do the same things.

As a congregation, we encourage a great diversity of ministries among our people. One friend referred to this as "spiritual entrepreneurship" or the practice of nurturing creativity and individual initiative as each member of the body develops a special place of ministry.

With the individual ministries and the diversity of those ministries in mind, what are we supposed to do collectively? We are to streamline our ministries so that we make the most of our time together and capitalize on those things we do best when gathered together. Targeting those ministries and then resisting the urge to embrace all the others available becomes a delicate process requiring the utmost discernment and discipline. We place a high value on doing a few things very well and not getting ourselves spread too thin by doing too much. The danger is the tendency to add on new ministries, rather than improve the ones to which we are already committed.

Each time an idea for ministry is presented, we must remember the important value of having a streamlined, targeted approach to ministry. We may need to give up something to add something new. We may need to expand the range of ministries once in a while. But in each case, we have a responsibility to measure what we are doing in the light of the value of keeping things simple and focused.

12. A WILLINGNESS TO CHANGE AND INNOVATE

Inertia is a dangerous condition for any congregation. The tendency of a body at rest to remain at rest, or a body moving in one direction to keep going in that direction, is inertia. When the body of Christ gets set in its way, it will often resist change, fight anything different, and dig in its heels at the slightest suggestion that something needs to change!

All change, even good change, represents loss, and so we can understand why folks resist it so often. Yet, we must also understand that change is what growing in Christ is all about. Since the day we first experienced that dramatic change from darkness to light, and from bondage to sin to freedom in Christ, we have been in the process of changing, growing, and becoming a new creation. Therefore, we value a willingness to change among God's people. Change is inevitable for a church that wants to grow to be more like Christ.

Buildings, ministry programs, orders of worship, musical tastes – not one is sacred and often must give way when more effective means exist to accomplish what Christ has given the Church to do. Stability brings security, but we must never allow our security to prevent us from accommodating ministry structures that would fulfill our calling more efficiently.

As we continue to grow in Christ, we must always ask ourselves if there is anything we are unwilling to do, any change we are unwilling to make, or any new direction we are unwilling to take in order to become what He wants. If we are to continue in fellowship with Him, any change and innovation He places before us will be a welcome one. We know that if He calls for change, He will use it to draw us closer to Himself. If we are unwilling, we will never grow to maturity in Christ. This last core value must guide our actions as a congregation until He comes again.

These are the twelve core values that have shaped and defined the unique personality of our ministry. As we embrace them, we have great hope that the Lord will continue to bless us with His Presence and the fullness of His joy.

The establishment of core values is an essential element for a healthy, vibrant church. By spelling out what your church values most highly, your congregation will also be able to retain a distinctive nature of ministry for generations to come. God is ready and willing to perform a masterful demonstration of His grace for any church that is truly open to Him.

Asking the Right Questions

The most impressive people I have ever met and who had the most immediate impact on my life were not brilliant speakers and writers, but those who knew how to ask the right questions. Operating with the assumption that not everyone is alike opens the door for us to explore new ideas, find new solutions to our own unique problems and challenges, and ask lots of questions so that we might learn what God wants us to know. In our naiveté, we sometimes try to find out what someone else has discovered and work desperately to make the answers they have found fit our situation. Instead, we would be better served if we found out what questions they asked. When defining the calling God has given each church, a "one-size-fits-all" approach to ministry just doesn't exist.

How then do we ask the right questions? What questions have been asked and answered in putting together the material in this book? Why were they important and what prompted them? What are the unique circumstances of your ministry that generate your own set of questions?

Without trying to present an exhaustive list of questions, I would like to provide you with seven sets of questions you might consider as you determine the unique character of your own ministry:

1.   How should I go about figuring out what a church really is? What authority will I use as the basis for answering that question? For example, will my source of authority be the traditions of my own denomination, the Bible itself, contemporary writers on the identity and calling of the Church, historical documents from earlier centuries in the life of the Church, or peers in ministry in my own network and community? Who or what will

have the final word if there is a conflicting opinion somewhere along the line?

2.   If I were to write down a purpose statement for my church based upon my current level of information and understanding, what would it say? What other secondary purposes or ministry categories might be added to clarify and sharpen the focus of that primary purpose statement?

3.   In each of the ministry categories I have listed as essential in the purpose statement, what evidence in the New Testament descriptions of the early church help shape my thinking and establish basic principles? I have listed below an example of this process involving evangelism and edification:

CATEGORY	OBSERVATION	INTERPRETATION	APPLICATION
Evangelism	Marketplace preaching in Acts 17:17	Message goes to where the people are who need to hear it and does not wait for unbelievers to show up at church.	The church should train its members to be effective communicators of the gospel out in the world among unbelievers.
Edification	Profitable teaching was done publicly as well as house to house in Acts 20:20	Provides consistent teaching that grounds believers in sound doctrine when firmly rooting new churches in Christ.	The church should make teaching a major building block for its ministry and teach that which is profitable (as Paul noted the Scriptures to be in 2 Timothy 3:16-17 and as the church in Acts 2:42 did in addressing the "apostles' teaching" to that early assembly).

The more extensively the process is followed, the better the picture of the biblical practices and principles of the Church become. In the early stages of writing this book, I spent months exploring every account I could find of what the Church did in the areas of worship, evangelism, and edification.

4.   Which of those areas appears to be the weakest in my own church? Are there areas we are not addressing at all? If so, is there some reason that needs to be addressed? What obstacle must be removed or priority realigned?

5.   What is my own area of preferred ministry? Is that reflected in the way I have invested in the ministry of the church I serve? Am I giving a balanced, biblical emphasis to every area noted in the Scriptures that is necessary to fulfill the calling of the church to completeness in Christ? What am I leaving undone that God has shown me must be addressed?

6.   Is the direction I am headed leading me to see the purpose of the church fulfilled, or will I need to make some significant changes in my own ministry to align myself and the church with a more biblical course? If I am not headed that way, what must I do to shift over to a new course? When should I make the change? What will be the biggest obstacle I will need to overcome? What resources are available to overcome that obstacle and others like it that I can expect to find along the way?

7.   Are there resources already written that will help me think through more clearly than I would be able to do on my own? Where can I find them? Who seems to be a few steps ahead of me in the growth process who might help me find some answers or formulate more specific questions?

One of the greatest things you can do for your church is to learn how to ask good questions. If you have spent much time studying the Bible, you already know that the best way to "unpack" a passage is to ask questions that help to peel away the layers that hide its deeper truths. The same is true for understanding more about the nature of your ministry in the local church. Ask lots of questions and work hard not to assume that you already know the answers.

I have only mentioned a few questions to help you get started in developing your own questions. When I die, I want to still have a list of questions in my pocket that I am working on. For the Church to become what it should be, its members need to have a holy curiosity that generates questions as we seek God's best for the Bride of His Son, Jesus Christ. Asking the right questions can be a wonderful key to unlocking the treasures He has prepared for those who dare to know what He longs to reveal.

Most Frequently Asked Questions
About Elder/Deacon Structure

Throughout church history, many forms of government have been practiced by the Church. Most of them fall into three main categories based primarily on how churches define the various biblical leadership roles and offices: Episcopal, Presbyterian, and the congregational form of church polity. In an Episcopal form of government, a bishop outside the local congregation exercises authority over the churches under his charge. In a Presbyterian form of government, a presbytery composed of leaders from various congregations exercise authority over the churches under their charge. Within each church there is a group identified as elders, who make up the governing body (or session) of the local church under the supervision of the presbytery. Then there is the congregational form of government, which recognizes no human authority outside the local congregation. Within this form, the church operates as a democratic organization and determines its own leadership structure by usually identifying its leaders as either pastors, elders, or deacons.

Providence Baptist Church functions within the framework of a congregational polity and identifies the two primary offices of the church as elders and deacons. We also recognize and support the ministry of those who are called pastors. The following question and answer format included in this appendix is intended to explain why we have followed this course at Providence. Although not intended to answer all the possible questions you might have, it should provide you with a basic understanding of the biblical reasons behind our decision to do what we do. Should you find that other explanations of the biblical texts make more sense than these, we are not offended!

We believe that we have chosen the best course based on the pertinent biblical accounts, but we also know that anyone who insists that there is only one legitimate form of church government cuts with a finer knife than we find justified by biblical evidence. In some cases, it may be true that the right form does not guarantee effective spiritual leadership because the character of those in office does not match God's design. In other words, their form is right but their hearts are not! Conversely, others may have missed the best forms but have succeeded in finding the right kind of people; therefore, they are enjoying wonderful effectiveness in their church leadership. What a joy it can be when we follow God's design and our leaders have godly leadership qualities! Here are some of the most frequently asked questions relating to the biblical structure of the body of Christ.

1. What does the Bible say about the role of elders?

People are often confused by the different words used in the New Testament to talk about the biblical offices. Most of the time, the biblical offices are recognized to be *elders* and *deacons*. It is not always clear what those words really mean, whom they refer to, and what those who are called to these leadership offices are supposed to do. Perhaps that helps explain why there are at least three distinctive forms of church government in practice!

Much of the confusion arises over the words used for elders. In the New Testament, Paul and Luke use two distinct words to refer to the same position or office, and these words are often translated into English as "elder" and "bishop." In Acts 20:17, we read that Paul called together the *elders* [Greek word is *presbuteroi*] of the church in Ephesus and delivered a farewell charge to them. As a part of that charge, Paul challenges these elders to "be on guard for yourselves and for all the flock, among which the Holy Spirit has made you *overseers*...[Greek word is *episkopoi*] (Acts 20:28). So we find these leaders called "elders" in 20:17 and then "bishops, or overseers" in 20:28. Both words are used to identify the same group. Not surprisingly, this has confused many who would like to separate those two offices and give them distinct functions, and it has frustrated others who do not like having to deal with two names for the same group of leaders!

As if it was not confusing enough, Paul then goes on in Acts 20:28 to exhort these elders and bishops (overseers) to fulfill their calling by "shepherding [*poimaino*] the church of God which He purchased with His own blood." The verb translated here as "shepherd" is translated elsewhere as "pastor, tend, feed" when Jesus told Peter to "feed My sheep" (John 21:16 KJV). The noun form of this word is also found in Ephesians 4:11 where Paul identifies four groups of leaders God gives to the body of Christ: "And He gave some as apostles, and some as prophets, and some as **evangelists,** and some as **pastors** [*poimenas*] and **teachers**."

The question to bring to the table is whether elders and bishops (overseers) and pastors all refer to the same office according to the New Testament. For many years I had concluded that the three words were interchangeable when used to identify this biblical office. However, although I still think that is a possibility, the text does not support that conclusion as decisively as I originally thought. We will discuss this topic in more detail in the question that follows.

The words elders and bishops (overseers) refer to a specific office recognized by the Church and described in the Scriptures. Regarding the biblical understanding of this office, the Scriptures offer instruction and information in the following areas:

- Ordaining of elders (Titus 1:5 and Acts 14:23)

- Qualifications of elders (1 Timothy 3:1-7 and Titus 1:5-9)

- Duties of elders (1 Peter 5:2-3; Acts 20:28; 1 Timothy 3:2, 5, 5:17; Titus 1:9,11; Ephesians 4:12; and James 5:14-15)

- Various other references to elders (Acts 11:30, 15:4, 6, 23, 16:4 and 1 Timothy 4:14)

In addition to these specific points regarding elders and bishops (overseers), it is important to note that these words are always used in the plural form throughout the Bible. Nowhere does the Bible speak of any church with only one individual, whether a pastor, bishop, or elder, charged with exclusive responsibility for the flock. Instead, they were appointed to serve collectively as a team to function in leadership over the body of believers committed to their care.

2. What is the relationship between pastors and elders? Are they the same?

As we have already noted, there seems to be some confusion about this question. Although many have attempted to identify pastors as the elders of the church, no biblical mandate justifies such an effort. A careful study of the relevant texts (those referring to pastors as well as those referring to elders) calls into question whether or not all elders are called to the specific function of pastor/teacher as mentioned in Ephesians 4:11. Although they are expected to shepherd the flock in their role as overseer (Acts 20:28), it is uncertain that the fact that they are "apt to teach" qualifies them with the necessary spiritual gifts of teaching, exhortation, preaching, or other gifts associated with the calling to be a pastor/teacher of the flock. Similarly, the identification of the pastor/teacher as those called to equip the saints for ministry in Ephesians 4:11 does not necessarily mean that those who have been uniquely gifted for that ministry must be identified as those who serve as elders.

In our application of the biblical principles on this subject, we have chosen to bring together what we believe to be the best of both worlds. We have pastors who are not elders and elders who are not pastors. Because we have many pastors on our staff, we designate one of them to be the senior pastor who provides organizational accountability and gives directional consistency to the overall ministry. The other pastors are responsible to the senior pastor who provides oversight to their ministries. Therefore, the senior pastor represents the entire pastoral staff team by serving in the office of elder. In the organizational structure here at Providence, he is the only member of the pastoral staff team who functions in that capacity.

When the elders meet, the senior pastor is joined by the other pastors who play an integral part by participating in the meetings but not in an official voting capacity. By informing and advising the elders on ministry-related issues, they offer their unique insights and perspectives to the discussions and contribute to the process by which wise, informed decisions are made.

By having elders who are not pastors, a special depth and breadth strengthen this crucial ministry team. Although we make every effort to downplay the distinction between those called *lay leaders* and *pastors* by vocation, we have found that having elders composed primarily of lay leaders has brought a wealth of wisdom and experience to the spiritual leadership of our church. When the pastors and elders share the common vision and values of the overall ministry, a strong, unified leadership team will be in place as each group fulfills its calling and complements the ministry of the other.

3. **Are there really different functions for elders and deacons, or is the whole issue simply a question of semantics?**

As we have already discussed, elders are called to lead the flock and serve as overseers of the ministry of the church. Deacons are called to support the leadership of the elders by assuming various aspects of the workload. As a result, elders are then enabled to direct their attention more intently on the priorities set for them in the Scriptures.

The responsibilities of deacons are not specifically defined in the Scriptures other than the functional role of servant. Historically, they have been identified with the group of seven men in Acts 6 who were chosen from among the body because they were full of the Holy Spirit and wisdom. Therefore they were deemed to be worthy servants to assist the apostles and the church in making sure that the Hellenistic Jewish widows were not overlooked in the daily distribution of food.

Although these men are not called deacons and the church leaders were the apostles (not elders, bishops, or pastors), the servant role they assumed has become the model for the office of the deacons. Like the elders, they are to be men of sound spiritual character as noted in the qualifications set forth in 1 Timothy 3:8-13.

For all the points of discussion about the specific functions and names for the office of elder/bishop, the office of deacon stands apart as a fairly straightforward role within the Church, the role of a servant. However, many churches have expanded the role of deacon to take over the role of elder and diminished the role of elder, replacing it either with ruling pastors or supplanting it with ruling deacons.

The elders are given the responsibility for watching over and guarding the flock as those who will be called upon by God to answer for those entrusted to their care. The deacons, according to the Scriptures, are never assigned that kind of responsibility. Therefore, a clear difference is made in the Scriptures in the ministry of these two offices.

4. What are the obvious advantages to a church in making the change from deacon-led government to elder-led government? In other words, why make any change?

The most obvious answer to this question is that we return to the apparent structure of the New Testament church as we see it described in the Scriptures. Both in terminology and function, this change will follow more closely with what the Word of God says. Secondly, it alleviates a tremendous burden often placed on deacons and pastors. Presently, the deacons are forced by necessity into the unenviable position of serving a dual role, performing the duties of both offices.

Thirdly, the plurality of elders provides a check and balance, serving as a safeguard to the tendency of one leader to assume an autocratic role of lording his position over the people (1 Peter 5:3). When the elders function as they should, they will operate as one unit, having sought together the heart and mind of God on every issue they consider. Since they will operate on a consensus basis for their decision-making, no one elder can dominate the life and ministry of a church by an assertive personality or persuasive leadership style. The Church is, therefore, protected from unsound leadership by selecting as its elders only those men of God who meet the biblical qualifications and who will act responsibly in their respective roles of leadership.

5. **Will this structure change the church from congregational government and establish a government in which the elders "rule" the church?**

This is perhaps one of the most frequently asked questions concerning the elder/deacon structure. The answer is very simply this: The church will still function within the structure of congregational government!

How is that possible? An elder-led form of church government and elder *rule* are not the same thing. Having elders does not force a church to abandon congregational polity. To assume that an elder-led church ceases to be congregational in polity would make it necessary to assume that deacon-led churches or pastor-led churches are no longer congregational in polity either. The elders are charged with the responsibility of leading the congregation, but the congregation still has the responsibility to hold the elders accountable for their leadership. A church does not need to be either purely representative in government or purely democratic. A middle ground can provide a way where there is responsible leadership from the elders and the opportunity for the voice of the congregation to be heard. Issues of significant impact on the life of the church should always be brought to the congregation for endorsement or veto by means of congregational vote.

However, a fine line must be observed between the submission of the members to their leaders (Hebrews 13:17) and the active role all members should take in pursuing a course of ministry consistent with their understanding of God's Word. Our desire is to surrender neither of these in governing the affairs of the church.

6.   Isn't it unusual for a Baptist church to make this kind of change?

First of all, this is not the right question to be asking. The identity of a church as Baptist must be a distant second to the church's identity as biblical. Denominational distinctives must never take precedence over what the Bible teaches. Where the two line up, great; where they do not, the biblical course must always be taken. Opponents to an elder-led approach to the government of a local congregation frequently identify the word elder with a Presbyterian form of government. Therefore, they conclude that embracing elder leadership abandons Baptist policy.

However, on the matter of elder leadership in the church, there is no divergence from historical Baptist polity at all. As a matter of fact, until recent church history, Baptists have had the kind of structure described here. Edwin Dargan,[1] professor of homiletics and ecclesiology at the Southern Baptist Theological Seminary at the turn of the twentieth century, wrote the following:

> "Deacons' ministries in modern churches tend to encroach upon and absorb that of the eldership....It is greatly to be regretted that there is any decline in the use of so venerable and scriptural a designation of the New Testament office, and a revival of its usage is greatly to be desired....It may be said that the plurality of elders in our earlier churches was a more scriptural order than that of today, and our churches would perhaps do well to reset this ancient landmark....Our churches today have

---

1 Edwin Dargan, *Ecclesiology: A Study of the Churches* (Louisville: Charles. T. Dearing, 1897) 106-107, 115.

discarded the plurality of elders. It is our custom now, even in very large churches, to have only one active pastor, or elder, while it seems clear that in the New Testament churches, certainly the larger ones, there were several or even many elders."

In 1859, Charles Spurgeon expounded many of the biblical passages relating to elders to his congregation at New Park Street Chapel, a Baptist church in London:

"In apostolic times, they had both deacons and elders; but somehow, the church has departed from this early custom. We have one preaching elder – that is, the pastor – and he is expected to perform all the duties of the eldership."[2]

As a result, the church soon implemented a plan to have elders **and** deacons. Spurgeon said, "I did not force the question upon them; I only showed them that it was scriptural; and then, of course, they wanted to carry it into effect."

Having heard from Dargan, a Southern Baptist, and Spurgeon, a British Baptist, we will conclude this question by quoting Earl Radmacher,[3] a Conservative Baptist and past president of Western Conservative Baptist Seminary in Portland, Oregon:

"The context of elders, in my past experience, has been Presbyterianism. Consequently, when I would hear someone refer to his church leaders as elders, I would automatically think of church government that is alien to that which is Baptist. I confess that I assumed this without ever doing a careful historical study of the early nomenclature of Baptist leadership (which used the term

---

2 Charles Spurgeon, *C. H. Spurgeon Autobiography: Volume 2: The Full Harvest, 1860-1892* (Carlisle, Pennsylvania: The Banner of Truth Trust, 1983) 74.
3 Earl Radmacher, *The Question of Elders* (Portland: Western Baptist Press, 1977) 1.

elders), or worse yet, without ever reckoning with the fact of the predominance in the Scripture of the use of 'elder' as a title of church leaders."

To summarize, there is absolutely nothing "un-Baptist" about having elders. As a matter of historical fact, it is a return not only to a more biblical designation but to one that is more in-line with the historical roots of many different kinds of Baptists.

7. What safeguards have been established to prevent domination of church affairs by a small group who may in later years deviate from the original intentions of the church?

The essential success of the move to an elder/deacon structure depends upon the selection of spiritually qualified men of God who meet the qualifications outlined in His Word. That is the most important safeguard there can be. Secondly, the qualifications must be reviewed not only by the congregation in their nomination and vote, but by the elders currently serving to ensure that each potential elder is examined as the Bible says he must be.

Thirdly, only the pastor serving as elder should remain in his position as elder more than the constitutionally prescribed term of office. He should remain as an elder as long as he is called by the body to serve in his capacity as pastor. At Providence, other elders are asked to serve four-year terms, after which they become ineligible for service for a period of at least one year before they can be renominated to serve again. Fourthly, they must still function within the context of congregational government in order to provide continued accountability.

8. What effect will this change have on the ministry of the deacons?

In a word, the effect will be radical! The deacons will be freed from all of their workload that pertains to the elders' duties, which currently consumes the majority of their time. The biblical responsibilities outlined for the *elders* include the following:

- To shepherd the flock of God (1 Peter 5:2; Acts 20:28; 1 Timothy 3:5)

- To be an example to the flock, not lording it over those allotted to their charge (1 Peter 5:3)

- To teach and exhort, thereby equipping the flock for ministry (1 Timothy 3:2; Titus 1:9; Ephesians 4:12)

- To refute those who contradict truth (Titus 1:9-11)

- To manage the Church in their role as overseers (1 Timothy 3:5, 5:17)

- To pray for the sick (James 5:14-15)

Deacons are not given specific responsibilities and duties in the Scriptures but are described as a valuable and necessary resource to be called upon as needed for help and counsel by the Church. They are to be servant-leaders responsible for serving the Church through various kinds of shepherding ministries (such as counseling inquirers after worship services, interviewing new members, serving the Lord's Supper, or providing leadership for benevolence ministries). Unlike the elders, the deacon role does not involve any governing or managing duties.

In summary, let me turn again to Earl Radmacher for a final assessment of this subject:

> "Regularly the Scriptures give the church a responsibility together with commensurate authority for conducting their business, i.e. choosing officers (Acts 6:3, 5; 14:23), exercising discipline of its members (Matthew 18:15-17; 1 Corinthians 5:4-5, 13; 2 Thessalonians 3:6, 14-15), sending missionaries (Acts 13:2-3), etc. This does not mean that

these churches may not delegate the managing of much or most of their daily activities to those elders whom they have chosen to rule over them, but it does mean that the congregation never relinquishes ultimate authority. And if it should happen that the elders as a group act irresponsibly, the congregation, in assembly, would need to bring them to account.

"At this point, therefore, it may be well to carefully distinguish between congregational government and congregational authority. The congregation has the authority to conduct all of its business in session, as it chooses; but this would make meaningless the choosing of elders and deacons. Obviously, the special qualifications required by Scripture for these offices presume special spheres of leadership. Therefore, the congregation must be careful not to destroy their own efficiency and effectiveness by becoming immersed in the managing or governing for which they have elected spiritually qualified leaders, and the leaders must be careful not to usurp authority for themselves which rightfully belongs to the congregation as a whole. Their governing is by guiding, not by directives. I believe that this balance can be preserved when the leaders lead by love, teach by example, and when the congregation exercises proper submission to those whom they have chosen in submission to the Word of God and the Spirit of God. Surely the balance is portrayed in Hebrews 13:7 and 17. May God help us to find it in practice."[4]

It is likely that some may question your church's decision to adopt an elder/deacon structure. However, it is quite clear that biblically, historically, logically, and practically such a structure will enable the body of Christ to fulfill its ministry more effectively and efficiently for the privilege of functioning under His authority and serving together in His Name.

---

4 Earl Radmacher, *The Question of Elders* (Portland: Western Baptist Press, 1977) 10.

Study Guide

PUTTING PRINCIPLES INTO PRACTICE

Whatever you have learned
or received or heard from me,
or seen in me – put into practice.
Philippians 4:9

Lesson 1

The Roots of a Healthy Church
(Introduction, Chapters 1, 2 and 3)

1. Why was the Church "not created for the sake of its members or even for the good of the human race" (pp. 8–9)? Why was the Church ordained (Revelation 19:7)?

2. What are some signs of unhealthy churches (pp. 9–12)?

3. In what ways did Jesus Christ demonstrate His commitment to the Church (Ephesians 5:25–27)?

4. What are some of the practices of an anthropocentric church (a church focused on man rather than God)? How can these practices put the spiritual health of the body of Christ at risk (pp. 9–10)?

5. How can good concepts such as "seeking God's best" and "striving for excellence" sometimes be counterproductive to true growth (pp. 9–10)?

6. Read Jeremiah 29:11 and Proverbs 29:18. What do you think is the connection between the "plans" of the Lord and the "vision" of the Church (pp. 11–12)?

7. Review the core values identified in the appendix titled "Core Values of Providence Baptist Church" (pp. 205–219). Which ones would you like to learn more about?

8. Why are no two churches alike (pp. 19–21)?

9. Read 1 Corinthians 12:11–24. How does this passage contradict the frequently held belief that some parts of the body are more important than others?

10. Define in your own words the characteristics of God's Word mentioned in the following passages: 2 Timothy 3:16, 1 Peter 1:25, and John 17:17.

Lord, give me wisdom as I search for your unchanging principles and apply them in an environment of diverse and gifted people in the body of Christ, the Church. Open my eyes to Your Word and show me where You would have me change my perspective and actions. Thank you for the truth and grace found in Your Word.

Discussion Questions

1. What are some of the interesting or funny experiences you have had when visiting different churches?

2. What are several misconceptions about the Church (pp. 8–12)?

3. Why are biblical principles important in determining a church's direction?

4. Why is it important for the pastor, church leadership, and church membership to be moving in the same direction?

5. In what ways did these first two chapters in *Firmly Rooted, Faithfully Growing* challenge your beliefs about the Church?

Lesson 2

The Roots of a Healthy Church
(Introduction, Chapters 1, 2 and 3)

1. Why are healthy roots important for the Church (pp. 25–26)?

2. Read Colossians 2:6–7 and restate it in your own words.

3. How does Ephesians 1:22–23 portray the relationship between Christ and the Church (pp. 26–27)?

4. What does 2 Timothy 3:16–17 say about God's Word?

5. If religious activity is done without the enabling power and joy of the Holy Spirit, what may be missing (Romans 8:5–9)?

6. Read 1 Timothy 3 and Titus 1 and list the qualities expected of those in spiritual leadership.

7. What are some characteristics of godly leaders, and how does godly leadership affect the rest of the body of Christ (pp. 28–29)?

8. Read Colossians 3:1–2 and reflect on these words of the apostle Paul. What should our priorities be?

9. Studying God's Word and applying it to your life is the best way to make sure your priorities align with His priorities. What three methods can you use to discover His goals and purposes in the Bible (p. 32)?

10. Review Providence's purpose statement and comment on which area you hope to learn more about (p. 33).

Lord, guide me to a closer walk with You through an understanding of Your Word. Give me ears to hear what You are saying and feet to go where You are leading me in my home, job, and church. Help me to understand Your purposes for my activities with You, with those who do not know You, and with those who already know You. Lord, I ask that you also give me the courage to change my priorities.

Discussion Questions

1. Have you ever been involved in an organization that had lost its sense of purpose? What was it like?

2. Why have many churches developed ministries that have become "busy" but "unfruitful"?

3. What are some things that can divert us from becoming what Christ wants us and the Church to be?

4. Why is it important to determine "why" we must labor in a ministry area before we determine "what" we are going to do in that ministry area?

Lesson 3

Growing in Exaltation
(Chapters 4, 5 and 6)

1. In Isaiah 43:1–7, God is speaking to His people, those He has redeemed. Why did God say He created those who are called by His name?

2. According to Psalm 104:31–34, how do believers give God glory?

3. Read John 7:38–39. In what ways does Jesus illustrate the new life within a believer, and Who is its source?

4. Review John 16:13–14 and describe how Jesus says the Holy Spirit will lead you.

5. Read the following passages and list the reasons why Jesus is worthy of all worship and praise: 1 Timothy 2:5–6, Colossians 1:15–18, and Revelation 5:6–14.

6. God interacts with those who worship Him. One of the most glorious worship experiences of corporate worship ever recorded in the Bible was the dedication of the temple built by King Solomon in Jerusalem. Develop a table with the following headings: Celebration, Contemplation, Confession, and Consecration. Then read 2 Chronicles 5–7 and list all the verses you can find that relate to these elements of worship.

7. How did God show His pleasure with the worship of the Israelites (2 Chronicles 7:1–3)?

8. Why do you sometimes find it difficult to fully enter into worship? Summarize what the Bible says in the following passages: Matthew 15:8, Psalm 66:18, and Matthew 5:23–24.

9. Jesus taught that the Father seeks people who will worship Him in spirit and in truth (John 4:23–24). How can you better prepare your heart to be ready to worship God in spirit and in truth?

10. "When God calls us to worship, He calls us to a comprehensive engagement of all that we are in order to glorify Him for all that He is in Christ Jesus. The fact that He abides in us, calls us the temple of the Holy Spirit, and refers to us as His sanctuary should clue us in to the magnitude of His design for the worship He seeks from His people" (pp. 51–52). What do these statements mean to you? How do they encourage you in your relationship with Christ?

Heavenly Father, I have so often failed to give you the glory You deserve! Forgive me for allowing the cares of this world to cloud my view of You. Guide me into Your truth so that I might think less about myself and more about Your character. Attune my spirit to Your Spirit so that I will be aware of Your presence and eagerly prepare myself for every opportunity to worship You.

Discussion Questions

1. Describe the most memorable worship service you have ever attended.

2. What does it mean to worship God in spirit and in truth?

3. Chapter Four describes different elements of worship: Christ-centered, consecrated, confessional, celebrative, contemplative, and comprehensive. Which element is often a part of your worship experience? Which element is harder for you to incorporate?

Lesson 4

Growing in Exaltation
(Chapters 4, 5 and 6)

1. Describe four elements of personal worship (pp. 56–57).

2. Read Psalm 25. What does the psalmist seek from the Lord (verses 4–5)? What does he say is the basis for his request from God (verses 5, 11)?

3. How can you prepare yourself for your personal time alone with God (Colossians 3:1–2)?

4. Describe the ways Jesus has made it possible for you to confidently approach God (Hebrews 10:19–23).

5. Read 1 John 1:9 and describe what God will do for believers who confess their sin to Him.

6. In Isaiah 12:1–3, the prophet describes several worshipful responses that come from a heart that knows the forgiveness God brings. What are they?

7. In Psalm 5:3, the psalmist gives us a glimpse into his daily time of communion and prayer with God. When does he pray? What does he do after he prays?

8. Psalm 145 is a beautiful description of both personal and family worship. Rewrite Psalm 145:4 in your own words.

9. What happens when one generation commends God's work to the other (Psalm 145:5–7)?

10. The most familiar passage describing family worship is Deuteronomy 6:5–8. List some modern-day parallels to the activities mentioned in verse 7.

11. Which of these times would be the best time for your family to set apart as a regular family devotional time?

12. In Colossians 3:14–17, Paul lists several benefits the Church receives when believers' hearts are focused on Christ when they gather to worship. What are they?

Loving Father, now that I have tasted new life through Your Son, I cannot be satisfied with anything else. I thirst to know You more. I want to hear and heed Your voice as I daily come to You in prayer and in the Word. May my times of personal worship spill over into special times of family worship as we talk together of Your works and Your ways. Fill my mouth with Your words, O Lord. May all I do culminate in praise and glory to You and to Your Son.

Discussion Questions

  1. Where and when do you like to have your quiet time? What essential tools do you like to have with you?

  2. What Christian books have you found useful for family devotional times?

  3. What successes or failures have you had with your family devotional times? What times work well for your family (mornings, specific evening during the week, etc.) and what other resources do you use?

  4. Discuss what might be meant by the "spectator mentality" and ways we can avoid it (pp. 60–61).

Lesson 5

Growing in Evangelism
(Chapters 7, 8 and 9)

1. Restate 1 Timothy 2:4–5 in your own words.

2. Write down the three areas of the evangelistic field and suggest a modern-day parallel for each one (pp. 72–73).

3. According to Acts 1:8, what will we receive from God when we become believers? For what purpose?

4. Review Acts 13:1–5. Describe how the believers prepared themselves for evangelistic service.

5. Read 1 Corinthians 1:18. Contrast the ways believers and nonbelievers view the message of the cross.

6. How are nonbelievers described in 1 Corinthians 1:18? Why?

7. "Accommodation has become such a primary value in our culture that it has replaced the integrity of maintaining the truth of the gospel" (p. 76). How are we tempted to accommodate the prejudices of nonbelievers or to deviate from the message of the cross (1 Corinthians 1:23)?

8. Read Galatians 1:6–10. Discuss the emotions Paul may have been feeling as he wrote these words. In what ways does the world distort the gospel today?

9. Review Romans 10:12–15 and reflect on Paul's urgency and his passion.

10. Read Romans 1:16. What is the greatest challenge you face in sharing the gospel? Why?

Father, I admit that I am sometimes ashamed of the gospel. Forgive me, Lord. Sometimes this world can be so intimidating. Yet there are people in my life who don't know or don't understand that You sent Jesus to die on a cross so that they could have eternal life. Empower me, Lord. Your Scriptures have challenged me and inspired me this week, and I know now where I must go and what I must say.

Discussion Questions

1. What good news has someone shared with you recently?

2. In what ways do we compromise the gospel?

3. Describe what is meant by a "sending mentality" (p. 77).

4. Discuss the kinds of barriers that prevent us from telling others about Christ.

Lesson 6

Growing in Evangelism
(Chapters 7, 8 and 9)

1. "The body of Christ is to be found in the world, among the lost, leading them to know Christ in the context of their daily lives, not by cajoling them to come to church meetings so that they can be saved" (p. 82). Read Acts 17:16–17 and describe how Paul demonstrated evangelism in action while he waited for his friends.

2. List some ways you could be more direct in reaching those who are lost.

3. Take a few moments and reflect prayerfully on the practical and verbal aspects of your witness (pp. 82–83). Are you stronger in one area than another? If so, how can you strengthen this area?

4. "If searching people want someone to show them rather than just tell them, we have to live more authentically, more genuinely, and with more integrity in the way we relate to others" (p. 92). Read Colossians 4:5–6 and record what it means to you to make the most of every opportunity.

5. What are six criteria we can use in developing our own approach to personal evangelism (pp. 90–91)?

6. List four commitments that must be a part of our personal evangelism strategy (pp. 91–93).

7. Read Colossians 4:2–6 and 1 Thessalonians 2:7–8 and describe how our personal evangelistic strategy can be a part of our everyday lives.

8. What are four specific ways the body of believers can become involved in missions (pp. 95–98)?

9. Read 2 Corinthians 8:1–5. Describe the Macedonians' attitude about giving toward missions. List several observations that strike you.

10. How do these passages especially challenge you (Matthew 18:19–20, Matthew 28:10, and Matthew 28:18–20)?

Father, I thank you that Your Scriptures are filled with directions and encouragement for sharing Christ with others. Lord, sometimes I do not feel as "gifted" as others to evangelize, and I worry about what to say or if I will offend someone. But Your Word is true, and the biblical principles are trustworthy. Remind me again of the importance of prayer with evangelism. Help me care deeply—as You do—about those who don't know You. Thank You, Lord.

Discussion Questions

1. When was the last time you were really lost? How did you find your way home?

2. Describe your reaction to the following statement: "Much of our message has been invalidated by our failure to live up to our claims that Christ makes a difference in our lives" (p. 92).

3. Read John 14:5–6. Would you consider sharing your personal testimony with your small group?

4. As a small group, what specific ways can we advance God's kingdom (going on a missions trip, organizing a community service project, etc.)?

5. Discuss this statement: "As Christians we have far too often misinterpreted the noise of their misbehavior and missed the cry of their heart . . . These are searching people, not mean people, not our enemies, not menaces to the cause of Christ, but searching people who need someone to show them the way to Christ" (pp. 88–89).

Lesson 7

Growing in Edification
(Chapters 10–13)

1. "We are a covenant people because we have been brought into His family (p. 102)." What did Christ offer as the promise of His new covenant (Luke 22:20)?

2. How does the new covenant differ from the old covenant (Hebrews 8:10)?

3. Jesus set the standard as a servant leader. Read Matthew 20:25–28 and John 13:3–8 and describe how He demonstrated servant leadership.

4. Read Acts 2:41–47 and list several ways Christians in the early Church celebrated and worshiped the Lord through large and small groups.

5. "A healthy church must maintain a careful balance between the two extremes of organism and organization" (p. 107). Read 2 Timothy 3:5–7 and describe some of the dangers of allowing either organizational extreme to flourish.

6. Read Romans 1:6–12. Note Paul's tone and greeing to these people he had never met. How does this change your view of your extended family in Christ?

7. According to Romans 8:17, what do we share as members of Christ's family?

8. Name three things needed in order for believers to be equipped (pp. 113–115).

9. How does God intend to carry out His plan for each of His children (2 Timothy 3:17, Ephesians 4:11–12)?

10. What should our personal goals be according to Ephesians 4:15–16?

Heavenly Father, thank you for sending Your Son to make a way for me to become part of your eternal family. Thank you, Lord Jesus, for Your loving example of servanthood and sacrifice. Make me aware of those who need encouragement and help me make Your church family here a welcoming place.

Discussion Questions

1. Have you ever been in someone's home and felt uncomfortable? Why?

2. "Regardless of where a believer goes in this world, family is always near" (p. 108). Do you have an experience that relates to this statement?

3. Read 1 Corinthians 12:20–27 and discuss why God wants every member to be a minister and not just pastors and teachers.

4. What can you do to help your church be a more welcoming place?

Lesson 8

Growing in Edification
(Chapters 10–13)

1. How we can edify each other in prayer (Acts 2:42, 4:31; Luke 11:1–4; Nehemiah 9:2–3; 1 Chronicles 29:10–20; and 1 Thessalonians 5:17)?

2. Why are relationships important to God (p. 123)?

3. What are some ways we can strengthen our relationships with one another (Colossians 2:2–5; Hebrews 10:24–25; Ephesians 4:1–3, 11–16; and 1 Thessalonians 3:10–13)?

4. List several ways we can edify one another through the ministry of instruction (pp. 126–127).

5. How did the early believers in Berea avoid the danger of insufficient instruction and false teaching (Acts 17:11)?

6. "Far too many Christians are willing to accept the benefits of belonging to the body but are not willing to offer themselves in service to the body" (p. 130). Which groups of people especially need our care and how should we serve them (pp. 130-131)?

7. Why is Christ pleased when we care for others (Philippians 2:3–7)?

8. Why is good stewardship important (pp. 131–133)?

9. How can you maintain balanced priorities in your life (Matthew 6:33)?

Lord, help me rearrange my life and bring it in balance with Your priorities. Forgive me for my selfishness, Lord, and help me serve others by encouraging them and caring for them. Make me a generous, godly, caring, and encouraging servant like You were when You were on earth.

Discussion Questions

1. Describe your relationship with someone who positively influenced your life when you were a young Christian.

2. How can we discourage a spirit of partiality within our small group and our church?

3. Review the table on page 134 and discuss why edification can deepen our relationship with Christ and with each other.

Lesson 9

The Godly Character of Ministry
(Chapters 14, 15 and 16)

1. "We can do the right things and do them in the wrong way. . . there [should be] a match between the character and the content of our ministry" (p. 140). What five characteristics should a church have to maintain structural integrity (pp. 140–141)?

2. Explain why a church needs to be structured for flexibility (pp. 141–144).

3. Why does God refuse to give us a "single blueprint as His grand architectural design for the effective church" (p. 144)?

4. What is a common pitfall when coming to a new church and how can it be avoided (p. 145)?

5. "Too many Christians have identified success in ministry as getting large numbers of believers together" (p. 146). Why should we resist identifying success in ministry in this way?

6. What are some of the dangers of an overcommitted life (p. 146)?

7. Is being equipped the final result God has in mind for us? Why or why not (p. 147)?

8. What does 1 Thessalonians 5:11 and 14 teach us about our accountability to each other?

9. Name two methods of building accountability and discuss ways these methods help us encourage one another (pp. 147–151).

10. "Our tendency is to follow the world's example of selecting leaders with characteristics that make them largely unsuitable for leadership in the Church" (p. 152). Discuss the differences between a natural leader and a spiritual leader (p. 153).

11. According to 1 Peter 5:2–5, why is servant leadership important (pp. 153–154)?

12. Everyone wants to be a leader, but we all must be followers, too. What is our challenge and responsibility as followers (pp. 154–155)?

Lord, may I be quick to be a vessel for Your use, sensitive to those You have given me the opportunity to serve, and faithful in praying for those with the task of being servant-leaders in my church. Show me where I can be a more effective and active servant of Yours.

Discussion Questions

   1. Describe an organization that drove you crazy because of its organizational style. Was it too disorganized or too rigid?

   2. What do you think Howard Hendricks meant when he said, "The Church must learn to distinguish between the unchangeable and what must be changed" (p. 143)?

   3. Discuss the positive aspects of accountability.

   4. Discuss the advantages we forfeit when we choose not to pursue a "shared ministry" (pp. 150–151).

Lesson 10

The Godly Character of Ministry
(Chapters 14, 15 and 16)

1. "We can appear to be operating at peak efficiency with everything in order, but in fact we may only be holding onto a form of godliness void of the substance and power of godly character" (p. 160). In 2 Timothy 3:5, Paul describes people who have a form of godliness but no power. What does this expression mean?

2. List five evidences of spiritual character (p. 161).

3. What should motivate us to be pure (1 Peter 1:15–16)?

4. How do the Scriptures describe purity (Isaiah 1:18, 2 Corinthians 11:2, and Revelation 21:18)?

5. Consider ways we are to evidence humility in our lives according to 1 Peter 5:6, Philippians 2:5–8, and Micah 6:8.

6. Discuss the dangers of not having a humble spirit (pp. 163–165).

7. The importance of genuine humility was certainly demonstrated by Jesus (Matthew 20:28). What are some practical ways you can demonstrate this humble spirit in your relationships at home, at work, with friends and family, and among other Christians?

8. "Once the grace of our Lord grips our hearts, how can we dare be anything other than wholly gracious to others?" (p. 166). How can we develop a gracious spirit (Ephesians 4:2, 2 Corinthians 9:8)?

9. Discuss some of the actions and attitudes a gracious spirit helps us avoid (pp. 165–166)?

10. What are some practical areas where you can "live out" your willingness to joyfully and humbly sacrifice your time, talents, and treasures in following Christ (pp. 166–168)?

11. "The Lord's definition of maturity is the only one that matters—regardless of how much we want to project the image of those who have already reached the goal" (p. 168). Discuss some practical evidences of maturity (Ephesians 4:13–16; Hebrews 5:12, 14 and 6:1).

12. "A bridegroom would never forget the insensitivity and carelessness of an unkempt bride who did not bother to prepare for her wedding day" (p. 179). How can we as His bride make ourselves ready (Revelation 19:7–9)?

Lord Jesus, I commit myself to a lifetime of being made ready by You. Help me to be firmly rooted and faithfully growing in You right up to the day You receive Your bride.

Discussion Questions

1. Does anyone have any interesting or funny wedding experiences?

2. What are the long-range ramifications of becoming satisfied with the outward trappings of ministry success and neglecting the inward track of spiritual growth?

3. Discuss some ways an increasing desire to be united with Christ in heaven could change your daily life.